THE A–Z
OF
DO-IT-YOURSELF
IN THE HOME

THE A-Z

OF

DO-IT-YOURSELF

IN THE HOME

By

HAROLD AND ELIZABETH KING

Illustrations by
Stanton Phillips

PAPERFRONTS

ELLIOT RIGHT WAY BOOKS
KINGSWOOD SURREY UK.

Every effort is made to ensure that Paperfronts and Right Way Books are accurate, and that the information given in them is correct. However, information can become out of date, and author's or printers' errors can creep in. This book is sold, therefore, on the condition that neither Author nor Publisher can be held legally responsible for the consequences of any error or omission there may be.

Made and Printed in Great Britain by
C. Nicholls & Company Ltd,
The Philips Park Press, Manchester.

CONTENTS

LIST OF ILLUSTRATIONS

Page

ACKNOWLEDGEMENTS

The Authors and Publishers acknowledge, with thanks, help from the following:

Black and Decker Limited
Crown Decorative Products Limited
Econa Parkamatic Limited
Glynwed Foundries Limited
H & R Johnson Limited
Key-Terrain Limited
Myson Group Limited
Pilkington Brothers Limited
Rentokil Limited
Richardson & Starling Limited
Stanley Tools Limited
Walker-Crosweller Limited

ABOUT YOUR HOME

Becoming a home owner is a major step, but all too often, after the first excitement is over, you are faced with the fact that any structure, new or old, needs regular maintenance to prevent costly deterioration from weather and wear.

You may have bought an older property cheaply with the intention of putting it in order and modernising an old-fashioned kitchen and bathroom (too often black spots), renewing out-of-date plumbing or electrical wiring and installing central heating.

According to your time, budget and inclination, many jobs, that may seem at first daunting, can be tackled if the task is analysed and you work to a plan, using the correct tools and techniques and taking full advantage of the modern materials available. .

Systematic inspection and remedial action immediately something goes wrong may save you money later. The best time for checking for problems and carrying out routine home maintenance is in the spring, after the worst of the winter weather, and in the autumn, with a final check to make sure your home is as weatherproof as you can make it before winter.

When maintaining the exterior, the best order of work is to start at the top and work down. Check the roof for loose tiles or slates. Look at the mortar around chimney pots and the flashing round chimneys and dormer windows.

Flat roofs may need attention. Inspect rainwater gutters. These should be free of débris and firmly fixed. If made of metal, check for rust and either treat or replace badly

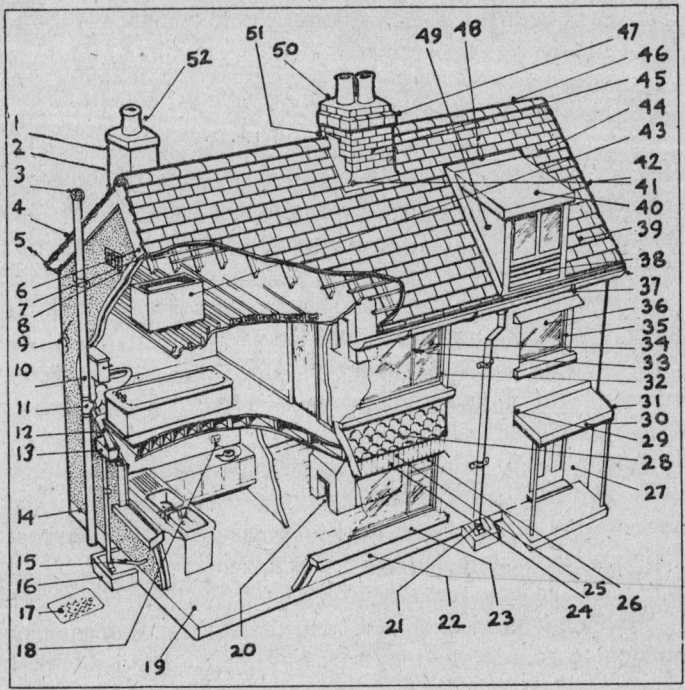

1. **Anatomical breakdown of the home.** The anatomy of your home
   — the "kit of parts" and where trouble is likely to occur. **(1)**
   Condensation stains (where flue not linked); **(2)** Chimney damp--
   proofing absent or defective; **(3)** Balloon over stackpipe to keep
   free of birds' nests; **(4)** Tiles decayed, cracked or missing; **(5)** Soffit;
   (6) Bargeboarding; **(7)** Tile undercloak; **(8)** Airbrick — keep free; **(9)**
   Cracks due to drying out of surfaces or sulphate attack; **(10)** Soil
   stackpipe; **(11)** WC branch connection; **(12)** Bath waste-pipe; **(13)**
   Waste hopper head; **(14)** Damp-proof course or air brick blocked or
   missing (in conditions of penetrating and rising damp); **(15)** Kitchen
   waste-pipe outlet; **(16)** Trapped yard gulley; **(17)** Manhole inspection cover (check in good condition); **(18)** Electric wiring and points
   — check at least every five years; **(19)** Dry rot — inadequate
   underfloor ventilation: also check for woodworm; **(20)** Fireplace —
   check condition of fireback and chimney draught (in the case of

damaged sections. A leaky gutter or downpipe can allow water to seep into the brickwork and very soon you will have tell-tale damp patches inside your home.

Timber or tile cladding may need attention. Replace any loose tiles and treat timber cladding with a timber preservative or repaint it.

Badly fitting doors and windows let in draughts and damp. Check that frames fit well, that timber is sound or that metal frames are rust-free. Also look for cracked glass or loose putty. Check the condition of all paintwork.

Brickwork may have become porous or pointing needs renewing, or areas of rendering may "blow" and break away from the wall. Ensure that air bricks are not blocked or obstructed. Inspect paths and the driveway for cracks and damage.

Make sure that gulleys and drains are not clogged and that manholes and drainage inspection points are easily accessible. Cracked manhole covers must be replaced for there is otherwise a danger to health.

Other maintenance checks indoors include plumbing and heating, looking for signs of damp, wet or dry rot and

---

smoky fire); **(21)** Rainwater downpipe shoe; **(22)** Check beneath sills – timber sill drip groove should be unblocked; **(23)** Check condition of sill and for gaps between sill and brickwork; **(24)** Soldier arch above window; **(25)** An alternative is a concrete lintel; **(26)** Window-frame head; **(27)** Surfaces likely to be marked if in light, vulnerable colour; **(28)** Tile-hung cladding; **(29)** Porch flashing; **(30)** Porch; fascia; **(31)** Porch offers door protection; **(32)** Jamb; **(33)** Mullion; **(34)** Transom; **(35)** Fanlight; **(36)** Fixed light; **(37)** Guttering – called rainwater goods or RWG; **(38)** Dormer face cladding; **(39)** Check beneath tiles that timbers are structurally sound; **(40)** Eaves dormer; **(41)** Tile verge; **(42)** Apron flashing; **(43)** Cold-storage cistern – check this is lagged; **(44)** Insulation in roof rafters where habitation in loft; **(45)** Chimney stack; **(46)** Ridge tiles; **(47)** Chimney corbel; **(48)** Soaker (flashing beneath tiles); **(49)** Cheeks of dormer; **(50)** Chimney flaunching; **(51)** Stepped flashing; **(52)** Chimney pot.

maintaining the standard of general decoration. This is important if your home is to be a pleasant place to live in.

Planning is the key word when undertaking any home repair job or alteration. Obviously, some jobs may be so urgent that they have to be done immediately, but ideally try to plan your work scheme to suit the weather conditions. Working outside in frost, wind or rain can be dangerous and weather may attack many of the materials you use.

Equally, big tasks like replacing windows, altering heating or plumbing and knocking down walls, should be left until the warmer months and you will have more daylight hours in which to work.

Damp conditions and poor natural light will affect most jobs undertaken during winter months. Even interior painting and paper-hanging are better carried out in good natural light and dry conditions. There are, however, many indoor jobs you can tackle during the winter months.

Avoid repainting during wet, frosty or very hot conditions. Ideally, exterior painting should be done during late spring or early autumn. Frost, dew and rain will all affect unprotected wood adversely. Hot sun will cause newly applied paint to flake and blister.

The diagram showing the "anatomy" of your home contains a variety of terms with which you may not be familiar. Refer to this "identikit" whenever you want to check any point or to pin-point the areas of possible trouble.

Materials and tools for home repairs can be bought, as appropriate, at builder's merchants, good hardware stores and DIY stockists.

A–Z OF DO-IT-YOURSELF

ACCESS

Many of the jobs you will want to tackle around the home, such as interior and exterior painting, roof and chimney repairs and so on, require good access equipment. Never skimp on using specialist equipment, for it is always better to be safe – not sorry afterwards!

Doing it the correct way is not only safer but also saves time, and you will work better. A "lash-up" arrangement may appear to cut corners, but, in the long run, may take longer to manoeuvre and be fraught with hazard!

The most common type of access equipment is the ladder. These are made in either aluminium or of timber. Aluminium ladders have the advantage of being light to carry and easy to maintain but are more expensive than wooden ones. Always take care when working near an overhead domestic electricity supply, for aluminium will conduct electricity.

The rails of wooden ladders are usually made of fir, hemlock, pine or spruce – all straight-grained timbers. Ash or oak are used for the rungs. Inspect any ladder carefully before use. Check ropes on an extension ladder and on timber ladders look for rotted rungs and joints that may have worked loose.

Never paint a ladder as this may disguise defects. However, it is a good idea to use a clear timber preservative or varnish to protect the wood.

Always store a ladder under cover. Not only will this protect it, but it will not be an invitation to thieves to use it to break in! Either hang it, secured, on wall-mounted brackets and covered over, if outside, or with a timber ladder, store in the rafters of a shed or garage where air can circulate.

To put a ladder up, first position the foot against the wall, hold with your hands outstretched over your head, then push it upright by working your hands down the rungs. Pull out from the bottom until the ladder is at an angle of about 70° to the wall, or roughly a quarter of the height of the ladder. The ladder once in the correct position should sit squarely to the structure.

Always secure the ladder firmly. Tie one of the lower rungs to a convenient projection or place a sack of sand behind the uprights to stop slip. Prevent backward slipping by driving two stakes into the ground, tying the lower rungs to these with a stout cord. On soft ground, use a timber board, tilted forward, so that the ladder does not slide away from the vertical surface.

Side-slip can be prevented by tying a rung to an eye hook fixed into the fascia board. Never tie to or lean a ladder against guttering. This is unsafe as the guttering may give way. Use a ladder stay which stands the ladder away from guttering where you cannot fix at the top. One end of the stay slots over the rungs, the other rests against the wall.

There are a few simple safety rules to observe when using a ladder. Always wear shoes, not boots, so that you can "feel" the rungs under foot. Do not climb in wet, icy or windy weather. You will find that all ladders tend to whip as you climb. This, however, is nothing to worry about.

Materials – brushes, clothes and glasspaper – can be put in your pockets but sharp tools, such as chisels or paint scrapers, should be carried in the hand so that they can be flung clear if you slip.

When you climb keep your eyes on the wall in front of you. If you look down you may feel giddy. Once working, keep one hand on the ladder at all times, stay within your

2. Ladders. Never allow a ladder to rest on a guttering or any moveable surface. Lash the ladder at the top and the bottom and position the base on a firm board, which is pegged and lashed.

centre of gravity and do not be tempted to stretch out on either side. If an area is not easily within reach, get down and reposition the ladder; it is both easier and safer!

Never stand on the top rungs — four rungs down is the minimum safety position.

For general use, a 4.3m ladder is quite sufficient, though other lengths are available. Over 3m, extension ladders are normally rope-operated. Always allow a two-rung overlap between the sections of a 4.3m ladder and three rungs on longer ladders.

If you need to work on the roof, use either a cat ladder or crawling boards. Crawling boards have a headboard, a top section, to which you can add extension lengths. Where crawling boards are used do not work from a ladder; use an access tower, it is much safer.

A cat ladder, a wooden ladder with an angled lip at the top which fits over the roof ridge tiles, may be used with a ladder or access tower as shown in fig. 2. Make sure the cat ladder is fixed firmly, if possible, to a firm point, such as a chimney.

A scaffolding platform or access tower is made up of lightweight tubular sections which slot together to make a framework to the height you require. The maximum height possible is 9.6m. The platform size is usually 2.4m × 1.2m.

3. Access tower. Is quick to assemble, light and portable and makes life at the top both easier and safer. Firmly lash any ladder used to tower.

The height of the tower should, ideally, not be more than three times the dimension of its base.

It is important to fit toe boards, timber upstands – which should be supplied – round the platform as this stops tools from accidentally being knocked over the side and becoming earth-bound missiles! You can either climb up the sections to the top or use a ladder lashed to the tower.

It is better, easier and safer to work from a platform tower, for you can have all your tools and materials with you and both hands free. Towers are quite mobile as they can be fitted with lockable castor wheels. Adjustable feet may be used to accommodate differing ground levels.

Where you need access at lower levels, a 1.8m step ladder in timber, aluminium or steel will be adequate. Again, always check for signs of wear and damage and never use a doubtful ladder.

Indoors, for ceiling work or reaching awkward high areas such as stairwell walls, a combination ladder and staging system will be invaluable. These may be used as trestle and staging, section ladders, a two-sided step ladder, or each section can be used separately.

Platform steps, which are similar to the usual step-ladders, have a platform at the top.

Whatever job you tackle around the home requiring access, there is a variety of equipment available to hire or buy that will make the job both easier and safer.

If you hire, of course, check that the equipment is in good repair. Check for damaged ladders as suggested earlier and look for rusty scaffolding or split boards. Reject anything that appears suspect.

ADHESIVES

There are many construction and repair jobs both inside and outside the home that involve using adhesives. Always use the correct adhesive for the material to the manufacturer's instructions.

For good bonding, work in a temperature of at least 16°C. Make sure that all surfaces are clean, grease-free and dry. Many glues are flammable or toxic, and should be used in a well-ventilated place.

Wall-coverings	— *Starch flour or water-soluble cellulose paste* (*Use a heavy-duty fungicidal paste with non-porous wall coverings, such as vinyls or in areas subject to high condensation*)
Fabric (unbacked)	— *Thick PVA or latex-based*
Fabric (paper-backed)	— *Generally heavy-duty wallpaper paste*
Cork	— *PVA*
Polystyrene (sheet or ceiling tiles)	— *Rubber resin, natural latex*
Ceramic floor tiles (interior)	— *Flexible, rubber-based*
Ceramic floor tiles (exterior)	— *Contact; epoxy-based resin*

Rubberised floor tiles, PVC floor tiles, felt- or asbestos-backed PVC, linoleum tiles	— *Rubber or synthetic-based*
Cork floor tiles	— *Contact*
Wood-block or veneered flooring (on screeds) (on suspended floors)	— *Rubber-based* *Flexible, latex-based*
Wood panelling	— *Flexible, gap-filling; synthetic rubber-based; contact*
Carpeting/joining seams	— *Latex-based*
Woodworking and general repairs	— *PVA*
Wood joints (cramped)	— *Casein glue*
Tight-fitting wood-joints (cramped)	— *Animal glue*
Laminates	— *Contact; synthetic resin; epoxy-based*
Quick household repairs and interior woodwork	— *PVA*

Small repairs to china and glass or for metal-to-metal fixing	— *Epoxy-resin*

Small repairs to articles (such as broken china)	— *Cellulose paste*

BRICKS AND BRICKLAYING

Laying bricks is a technique which needs some practice but provided you observe a few simple rules, the skills are not difficult to acquire.

For jobs such as building a stone fireplace or laying ornamental garden walls some irregularity can be tolerated. With practice and confidence your work can take on a professional look!

You will require a good bricklaying trowel, a small pointing or "dotter" trowel, with a club hammer and bolster, a long spirit level, a straight edge, a wire brush, a shovel, a pair of bricklayer's pins and a few metres of cord.

Use a "lean" mortar — 1 part of cement to eight parts of soft sand, plus one part of lime or plasticiser. This makes the mixture "fatty" and easier to use.

The coarser the sand, the "hungrier" it is, needing lime or plasticiser. A squirt of washing-up liquid does as well as a proprietary plasticiser.

You can control the mortar colour by choice of sands or proportions used in the mixture. Avoid a "strong" mixture with a high proportion of cement. A lean mix allows the correct degree of expansion of brickwork, and joints will not crack.

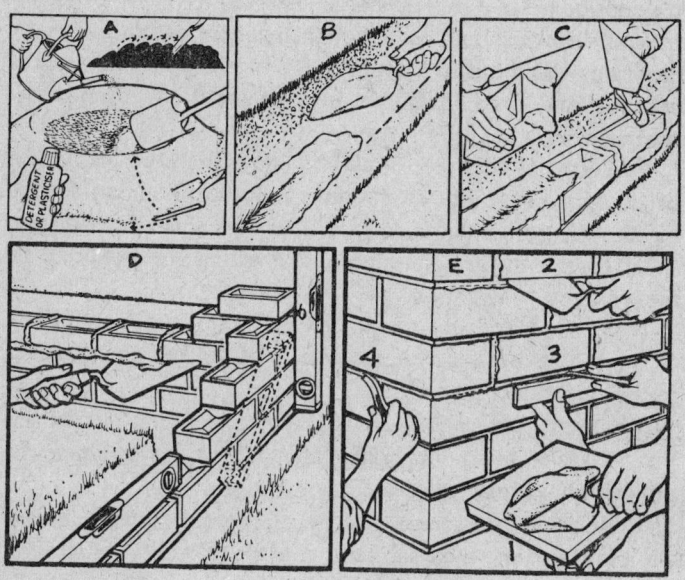

4. Bricklaying.

A. Well mix the constituents dry, form a crater and pour in water sparingly from a can. Mix to plastic consistency.

B. Distribute a thin, even layer of bedding mortar to the scratched datum line.

C. Lay the bedding course, "buttering" the brick ends to form cross-joints, then tap into place with the trowel handle.

D. Build up the quoins (ends) by "racking back". Work to a string line to ensure accuracy. Scoop off extruded mortar after tapping down bricks and return to spot board. Use the spirit level to check that levels are correct.

E. Pointing is the finishing stage. (1) Work from a hawk; (2) Use a small trowel to make a weathered joint; (3) Strike the joint neatly horizontally and vertically using the trowel tip. (4) Use a piece of bucket handle for pointing.

Mix on a "spot" board, following the methods suggested in the section on concrete on page 35.

Stack the bricks neatly along the working area but clear of the spot board to avoid mortar splashes.

Your bricks should be laid on firm concrete foundations or "footings". Dig out to a depth of around 225mm and pour in concrete and tamp down to a depth of about one brick below the surface.

The strip of concrete should be wider than the width of a brick. Make sure that the footings are level. You can do this by knocking in small stakes, at intervals, checking with the spirit level and straight-edge and levelling the concrete to these stakes.

If the site slopes, you will need to lay stepped foundations — at intervals build up an end course of bricks below ground to the extent of the gradient.

Concrete takes about 21 days to "cure" (completely set) but you can lay your bricks after a few days, when the concrete has gone "green".

First lay a thin screed of concrete, set up a string line on the building line, then scratch, with the trowel tip, a straight working line in the screed.

Do not allow mortar to harden on the blade of the trowel, for this roughened surface makes it difficult to pick up and spread the mortar. Thoroughly clean the blade after use.

Use the brick trowel to scoop up a pear-shaped wedge of mortar from the spot board. Hold the leading edge of the trowel downwards at an angle, cut a wedge of mortar from the board and draw it towards you. Scrape the board surface clean to provide a fully loaded, evenly balanced trowel.

Hold the trowel above the footings, tilt it downwards, then pull it back with a sharp movement; this spreads the mortar out evenly on to the concrete.

Spread the mortar with the tip of the trowel, using a sideways motion. This layer is called the bedding mortar; spread this to about 20mm thick. Make a continuous furrow in the mortar. Take care to preserve your working line.

Pick up your first brick, lay it accurately and tap it down gently with the trowel handle. Take the next brick, scoop up a small wedge of mortar with the trowel, and lightly "butter" the corners of the brick at one end to provide cross-jointing.

Lay the next brick against the one just laid. Tap gently with the trowel handle against it to squeeze out the surplus mortar, then strike this off with the edge of the trowel, and return to the spot board. Continue this procedure.

The mortar joins should be an even 6mm — both horizontally and vertically. If the joint is too thick, do not try to hammer this down with the trowel handle, but remove the brick and scoop out some mortar.

At a corner, similarly mark out screed rules in the concrete and lay corner bricks alternately at right angles to each other.

Build up the ends, or quoins, of courses first by "racking back" — laying one brick less in each successive course.

As the wall rises check that the perpendicular or vertical joints line up (called the "perpend"), and that all joins are even. Use the spirit level to maintain horizontal and vertical accuracy.

Work to a string line, using the bricklayer's pins. Insert these in the mortar joints at each end and "snag" the line over the top edge of the quoin. Ensure that the line is kept in good order.

For any wall longer than a metre in length, always use pins and line.

There are various "bonds" in bricklaying. Bricks laid with

the faces parallel with the wall are laid in "header bond"; laid with the head (or narrow end) parallel, this is a "stretcher bond". An alternate header-stretcher bond is called "English bond".

You may have to cut a brick in half to fit. Cut across the brick, it is called a "bat", and cut length-ways a "queen closer".

A bricklayer will cut a brick by striking it with the edge of the trowel. This calls for practice and it is much safer to cut bricks with a club hammer and a bolster.

Allow the bricks to dry, brush off any face mortar — but try to lay bricks cleanly — then point the joints. Follow the method outlined under repointing on page 27.

An ornamental wall may be finished off with capping; lay this as for bricks.

A wall, other than a low wall, longer than 3 metres, may require support piers. These are built up to form a block or pier, laid with alternate headers and stretchers, similar to construction of corner brickwork.

BRICKS AND BRICKWORK

The bricks and mortar of the home generally need little by way of maintenance, but problems such as spalled (crumbly) and porous brickwork or crumbling pointing has to be put right, for this can allow damp to penetrate inside and damage the fabric of the home.

Grimy brickwork can be freshed up by washing down with clean water, used with a stiff wire brush. If oily fumes have caused discolouration, add one part of bleach to four parts of water. Finally, rinse off with clean water. Take care not to splash yourself, but if you do, wash off at once with cold water.

Efflorescence, a chemical reaction within the bricks, produces an unsightly white crystaline deposit. This is brought to the surface by the action of the weather — rain and moisture. Remove as much of the deposit as possible with a stiff wire brush, then wash down the surface with a solution of spirits of salt. If you splash yourself, wash this off at once with cold water. Rinse well with rainwater — do not use tap water for, particularly in hard-water areas, this can cause the chemical reaction to recur.

You can also use neutralising solution which you apply to the surface with a brush.

Dull brickwork can be cheered up by using a colour wash.

Vegetable staining, as caused by vegetation growing against the walls, can be removed by brushing with a soft broom, then treating with a fungicidal solution. Mould or lichen is removed by applying a weak bleach solution to kill it, and brushing off a few days later.

Porous brickwork

Badly spalled bricks need chipping out and replacing. Porous brickwork can be treated by brushing or spraying on two or more coats of clear silicone fluid.

Rust stains sometimes appear in pointing — usually as a result of impurities in the sand. Chip this out, using a club hammer and a cold chisel, apply a rust inhibitor, then repoint.

Repointing

The joints or jointing between brickwork, particularly on older homes, may be crumbling and need replacing. This is called repointing. Rake out, using a club hammer and a plugging chisel, or you can speed up the job by using a routing head on a power tool. Use this at a slow speed and wear shatterproof glasses.

Tools needed are a pointing trowel to apply the mortar and trim off surplus, a hawk, which you can buy or make up from a 300 sq. mm of marine plywood with a short piece of broom stick screwed to the base as a handle, and a long wooden straight edge. You can trim an old kitchen knife to a slim blade to trim surplus mortar, this is called a "Frenchman".

There are several pointing tools which you can use to make up a variety of joints. You can also use a curved piece of metal bucket handle to "strike" or finish a joint.

There are three main joints — the flush, the recessed and the weatherproof joint. Recessed joints are usually used with rough-surfaced bricks.

Place polythene sheeting in front of the work area to catch mortar droppings. Work over an area of about a square metre at a time.

Brush down brickwork with a soft brush to remove any old loose mortar, then soak the open joints with clean water, using a paintbrush. This helps the new mortar to adhere.

Mix up replacement mortar on a "spot" board — a large piece of board — using a mixture of one part of bricklaying cement to four parts of soft sand. You may have to vary the mortar mix slightly to match existing sound pointing.

Once you have repointed the joints, trim off surplus from both horizontal and vertical joints, using the pointing trowel or the Frenchman, together with the straight edge.

The finishing touches can now be applied. The flush joint is made by allowing the mortar to become fairly stiff, then smoothing flush with a piece of sacking rubbed along the joint. Recessed joints can be made by finishing with a pointing tool or the piece of bucket handle. Recess the joint to a depth of about 6mm.

Weather-struck joints are generally used on exposed surfaces such as chimneys.

Form the verticals followed by the horizontals, using the pointing trowel. Slope the verticals to one side. "Strike" the horizontal joints so that these are recessed below the top of the brick and slightly overhang on the lower edge.

Settlement and shrinkage can be caused by faulty foundations or damage to these from tree roots. With large settlement cracks, you need specialist help. Repair shrinkage gaps between joints by repointing.

CARPETS

Carpet choice should be part of planned décor. When redecorating, never leave choosing a carpet till last. Colour, texture and quality, and choice between a plain or a patterned carpet, are all important.

A patterned carpet is best used with plain walls, or with wall finishes which are not too dominant. Plain carpets allow you a wider choice of scheme.

A light carpet can brighten up a dark room and make it appear larger. Browns, reds, oranges and yellows, all warm colours, will make a "cold", north-facing room feel warmer.

Long, narrow rooms will appear wider if carpeted with a striped carpet. A carpet with a large design will make a big room feel smaller and more intimate.

There are three main types of carpet — Axminster and Wilton, both woven and tufted, or non-woven carpets. Always buy a carpet suitable for the wear it will receive. These are labelled to show this.

Other than for backed carpets, you should always use a suitable underlay. It will not only make your carpet feel more luxurious, but, most important, will help it to wear better. Use the type of underlay prescribed.

Though carpet-laying can be tackled, for an expensive carpet it is probably best to have this professionally laid. The principles are not complex, but there is a degree of acquired skill. It is easy to ruin an expensive carpet. Backed carpeting is easier to lay provided you use a lot of care.

When laying carpet, you use a tool called a knee-kicker or

carpet stretcher, which you can hire. The head of the kicker engages on the face of the carpet and stretches it over gripper pins, wood or metal battens with small spikes which engage on the back of the carpet. Fix these to the floor along the wall edges of the room.

It is important to stretch the carpet correctly; if pulled the wrong way, it will wrinkle and pull out of shape.

Carpet can be cut and joined along the back with a seaming tape. In doorways you can protect it with a metal edging strip, or edge woven carpets with binder tape. You may have to fit rising butts to door hinges. These lift the door as it opens, to clear the pile.

One type of carpet which can be laid without using traditional carpet-laying skills are loose-laid carpet tiles. These are usually produced in 450mm × 450mm squares and simply butt together. You can take up tiles and reposition them to equalise wear. Tiles can be cut through the back with a sharp handyman's knife.

You can make up tiles from cut sections — butted together and you literally will not see the join!

When measuring for a stair carpet, allow 450mm extra so that you can shift the carpet periodically to equalise wear. Move the carpet up about 75mm every nine months, then work back the other way. Lay the carpet with the sweep of the pile facing down the stairs.

Work from the bottom upwards. Carpet can be tacked or fixed with gripper strip, or you can use stair rods. Nail gripper strip into the angle formed by treads and risers, other than the bottom, and fit underlay pads.

Fix the end of the carpet to the back of the bottom tread, using an angled strip, and to the bottom of the first stair riser with a flat strip. Keep the carpet taut and stretch it over the nosing of the bottom stairs. Press into the first angled strip, then smooth the carpet into the teeth of the gripper. Work towards the top of the stairs and finally tack.

On bends or winders, tack in the slack at the narrow point to make a series of folds at the back.

Look after your carpets. Lift furniture and never push it. Use castor cups on the feet of heavy furniture to avoid "point" wear. Do not use a vacuum sweeper on a new carpet.

CEILINGS

A good ceiling surface is something to look up to! Generally, a sound surface only needs sponging over and repainting — dependent on how clean the atmosphere is. Smoke and kitchen fumes may necessitate fairly frequent repainting. Deal with cracks and holes as explained on page 153.

Distemper is little used now, and plastic emulsion paint is widely used for decorating large surfaces, such as ceilings. Never attempt to paint over distemper. The paint will merely flake off. All distemper must be thoroughly sponged off first.

Use safe access equipment when decorating — such as a firm scaffold board on trestles so you can walk along the length of the ceiling and high enough so that you can reach the ceiling with ease. You will work better and with less effort.

Cover or remove all furnishings so that you do not splash them. Paint with a large ceiling paint brush — the best you can afford — or use a roller and paint tray. Techniques are outlined in the section on painting.

Ceiling tiles

A smart ceiling finish can be produced by ceiling tiles of cork, polystyrene or wood fibre. The ceiling must be clean and sound — though tiles can be used to disguise minor cracks in plaster. You should, however, always repair larger ones, for these are points of stress and the ceiling can distend.

It is usually best to start tiling from the centre of the room to preserve symmetry. However, to avoid awkward edges, for it is unlikely that tiles will fit the room module exactly, adjust the centre, if need be, to produce the best balance. Mark datum lines at right angles (across the centre) — best done by twanging a chalked line against the ceiling — spread adhesive evenly to the back of the tile. Never apply just blobs for in the event of fire, the air gap would promote the spread of flame.

Wear cotton gloves when putting up polystyrene ceiling tiles to avoid marking them. Work outwards towards the edges of the ceiling and cut in to fit.

To ensure an accurate cut, place the tile to be cut over the adjacent tile in the last complete row. Do not stick that tile yet. Hold another tile on top and cut through the bottom tile using the edge of the top tile as a marker. The cut line on the bottom tile will fit the wall contour accurately.

Polystyrene is easily cut with a handyman's knife. Also cut in around ceiling light fittings.

Timber ceilings

A timber ceiling, fixed to a battened framework, consisting either of panelling or planks, can provide character as well as lowering a high ceiling. Concealed, recessed light fittings look effective with this type of ceiling.

Illuminated ceilings

An illuminated ceiling, consisting of aluminium angled strip and glass-fibre translucent panels, is easy to erect and also lowers a high ceiling.

Fluorescent lighting above the ceiling provides a shadowless, even spread of light.

The inner, lattice framework slots loosely together into a wall angle strip, fixed with masonry nails or screws.

The angle strip is easily cut to size with a hacksaw, while the panels are cut with a sharp handyman's knife. There is a choice of panel designs and colours.

CELLARS

Basements and cellars are either partly or completely below ground areas and may become damp — either rising damp, through floors, or penetrating damp, through walls.

In an older home, the floor may be laid directly on to the soil, and have no damp-proof membrane (DPM). Treat slight damp with a damp-inhibiting epoxy-resin liquid. In severe cases, you will have to lift the floor and lay a damp membrane such as a 500-gauge polythene sheeting or a liquid bitumen solution, brushed on to a sub-floor concrete base. This can then be screeded over.

It is almost impossible to eliminate all dampness but aim to prevent the damp spreading upwards. Remove skirtings and hack back damp plaster. Treat walls with a liquid bitumin solution or clad with a bitumen-impregnated, corrugated lathing. Fix with galvanized clout nails and plaster the surface.

Alternatively, batten the walls and clad with plasterboard or a decorative wall cladding. Treat the backs of the battens with a clear timber preservative.

An extractor fan will also help to keep the area ventilated.

Condensation will be cut if there is adequate heating, which will be essential if the area is to be used as a family activity room or workshop. It may be possible to use the space as a laundry room (but check access to pipe runs and plumbing supply), or to site a central-heating boiler.

Make sure that you have good lighting, particularly on access stairways, which to cellars may tend to be steep and narrow.

CEMENT AND CONCRETE

Concrete is the staple material for many surfaces – foundations, sub-floors, paths, drives and surrounds – though there are alternative surfacings you can use for paths and drives, such as bitumen, paving slabs, gravel, brick, shingle and crazy paving.

Avoid concreting in frosty or very hot weather or it will crack. On a very hot day, cover fresh concrete with sacking and keep this damp.

Mixing
Correct mixing of concrete is the key to success. If it is wrongly mixed, the surface may break up.

You need a firm mixing base, such as a large, clean piece of board or a flattened piece of corrugated metal. Do not mix on a concrete or decorative path, for this will stain and spoil it. The basic tool is a clean shovel, which must be kept clean at all times, for you cannot mix properly if it is encrusted.

Keep all the materials separate — sand, cement, aggregate — and measure out the quantities "dry". It is essential that the mixture should correspond with the requirements of the type of surface.

It is, in fact, a good idea to make up a simple wooden gauge box for measuring quantities accurately. This has no top or bottom. Mix the sand and aggregates thoroughly together, then add cement to the heap and mix until an even colour is achieved. Form this into a crater and add water. Always use a watering can — a hose will separate the materials and weaken the mix.

Turn the materials in, from the outside and mix thoroughly. Add water sparingly until the mixture is pliable and has a "plastic" look. Flatten with the back of the shovel and jab this in several times. If the mix is correct, these ridges will not "slump".

Repairs

Repairs to a damaged concrete surface may only require the hacking out of a crack and making good. Badly cracked surfaces — as a result of a too-thin concrete layer, defective hardcore or a wrong mixture — may have to be replaced fully.

To repair cracks, slightly undercut these, using a club hammer and bolster, and clean out thoroughly with a stiff wire brush. Apply a dilute mixture of PVA adhesive along the edges of the crack; this helps to bond the new concrete. Mix the repair concrete consisting of one part of cement to three parts of sand. Add a small amount of PVA adhesive to the mix. Push the concrete firmly into the crack with a pointed metal trowel.

Where the edge of a path or drive has broken away, remove all débris and make good, if necessary, the hardcore base. Hardcore should be "clean" — that is with a minimum of dust and plaster. Stake a stout board — this is called shuttering — along the edge and bond the edges of the existing concrete with PVA, then fill with concrete.

Tamp the new concrete with the edge of a board or the back of a shovel to remove air pockets. Finish off with a steel trowel, for a smooth finish, or a wooden float for a roughened finish.

5. Tamping concrete. A tamper compacts the concrete between the shuttering. This also imparts a roughened, non-slip texture to the surface.

New drives and paths

When laying a new drive or path, first remove the top soil and all plant life; make sure that you do not leave in roots which will wreck the drive after a time.

Allow, for a drive, about 100mm depths of hardcore and the same level of finished concrete. For a path, use half these quantities.

Place shuttering, consisting of stout planks firmly pegged, along each edge. The shuttering has to contain the weight of the concrete at the edges, so it has to be firm. Where a path or drive is adjacent to the home, make sure that it slopes away, so that rainwater is taken clear of walls and foundations.

Tamp the hardcore firmly down with a pounder or the edge of a stout board so that it is even and well compacted.

Spread concrete evenly between the shuttering and draw a long plank or a scaffold board across edgeways. To make this tamper easier to use, nail or screw on simple handles. Finally, tamp down with the board edge, using an up-and-down action to compact the surface and remove air.

On a length or width greater than 3m, it is best to incorporate a concrete expansion strip which reduces surface stress and prevents cracking. Either encase a creosote-soaked timber strip the depth of the concrete, or position a batten temporarily, remove when the concrete has almost set, then fill the gap with bitumen.

These are the mixtures for a variety of surfaces. They are given by volume. The first figure is cement, the second builder's sand, and the third is aggregate (gravel).

drives	*1:2½:4*
paths	*1:2:3*
shed bases	*1:2½:4*
bedding for	
concrete slabs	*1:9*
foundations	*1:2½:4*

Removing stains

Grease or heavy oil are difficult to remove, but first scrape away as much of the encrusted deposit as possible. Scrub the surface with detergent, then wash clean. You can also use a proprietary alkaline degreasing solution or car engine-cleaning fluid, afterwards washing the surface clean.

CENTRAL HEATING

An out-of-date central-heating system may cost too much to run and offer very limited efficiency. Heating has taken great strides in recent years, and it is now even easier to install your own heating system.

However, this section is intended to provide general guide-lines and not a detailed guide to heating installation. It is possible to get a full "kit of parts" from heating suppliers, backed up with a design service.

The advantages of microbore central heating over other systems, such as the standard small-bore system, are over-whelming. Modern low-water-content boilers cut the amount of water in the system, so you can have a very quick heat-up time and fast recovery of heat.

The much smaller amount of water you have to heat cuts bills — but it is important that you take care to ensure that thermal insulation is as good as you can achieve.

Microbore heating uses small pipes of only 6mm, 8mm or 10mm, compared with the 15mm, 22mm and, sometimes, 28mm used on small-bore systems.

Heated water is taken to the radiators or convectors from a central manifold. You may have one serving the whole house, or the number of outlets and the layout might work

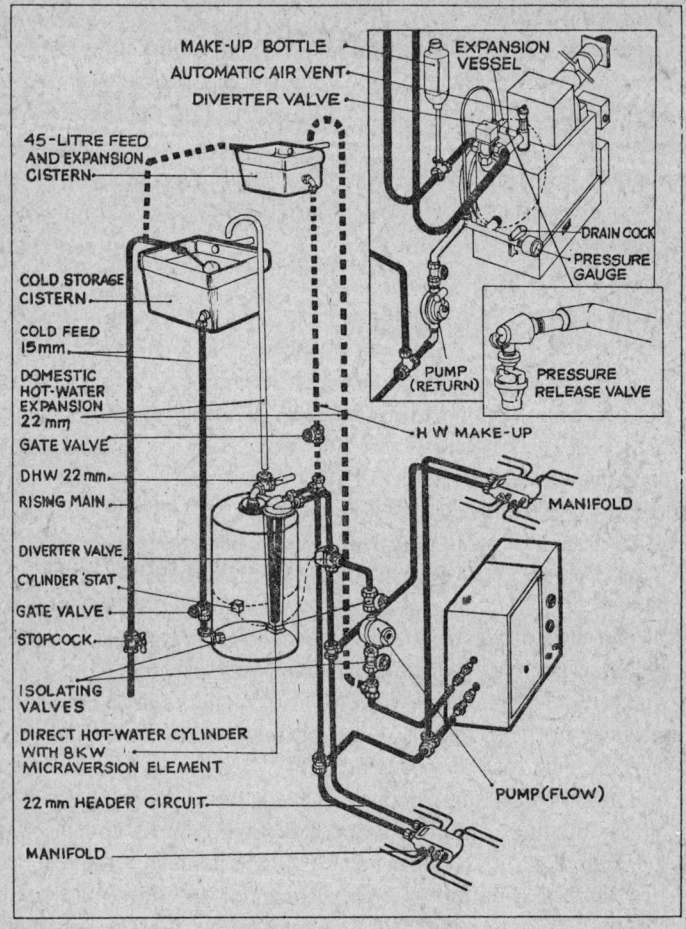

MAKE-UP BOTTLE
AUTOMATIC AIR VENT
DIVERTER VALVE
EXPANSION VESSEL

45-LITRE FEED AND EXPANSION CISTERN

COLD STORAGE CISTERN

COLD FEED 15mm

DOMESTIC HOT-WATER EXPANSION 22 mm

GATE VALVE

DHW 22 mm

RISING MAIN

DIVERTER VALVE

CYLINDER 'STAT

GATE VALVE

STOPCOCK

ISOLATING VALVES

DIRECT HOT-WATER CYLINDER WITH 8 KW MICRAVERSION ELEMENT

22 mm HEADER CIRCUIT

MANIFOLD

DRAIN COCK
PRESSURE GAUGE

PUMP (RETURN)

PRESSURE RELEASE VALVE

H W MAKE-UP

MANIFOLD

PUMP (FLOW)

6. Central heating. Schematic layout for a microbore heating system for both a sealed and an open type of installation.

better with two manifolds — one for upstairs and the other downstairs. If you have solid lower floors, you will need to fit a drop-pipe arrangement. Microbore pipes can be let into walls if need be.

With microbore heating, the domestic hot-water is pumped from the boiler. Small-bore systems frequently use natural or gravity (hydro-syphonic) hot-water circulation with pipes of 28mm diameter. This is wasteful on heat and means that the boiler has to be sized to take into account domestic hot-water needs.

On a microbore system, this is not really necessary, as you use a fast-recovery hot-water cylinder, so that pumped domestic hot water is rapidly re-heated without great demand on the heat output of the system.

A few simple heating mechanical or electrical controls are needed to control the operation of heating and domestic hot water.

There are two basic types of control — the motorised valve, which switches heating or hot water in or out, according to needs, and the three-port diverter valve, which usually provides a "priority" on either heating or hot water.

Another type of diverter valve shares the demands of heating and hot water, so that at peak demand times, both may be working at slightly lower levels — usually barely detectable.

Modern stowaway lightweight boilers can go almost anywhere — under worktops, in lofts and garages, cupboards or on an outside wall. They work in conjunction with high-head pumps which circulate the water quickly. Older, cast-iron boilers (known as high thermal-content boilers) hold a great deal of water, hence the heavy casing to keep in heat.

The modern lightweight boiler senses heat-levels more quickly because of its low water content, so controls work with greater precision, providing economic operation of the system.

There is far less fabric disturbance when installing a microbore system, and it is largely self-balancing, unlike a small-bore system. By following a few simple guide-lines you should experience little difficulty in installing. Balancing is the need to adjust the flow to radiators to allow an even heat output throughout the home.

You can choose most types of fuel. Microbore systems can be fired by gas, solid fuel or oil. Solid-fuel appliances have become very efficient — and the latest types of room heaters even consume the smoke content in a secondary chamber! You need to provide gravity or natural circulation to provide a "heat leak" when fitting fires without thermo-static control.

Gas and oil appliances can use a balanced or conventional flue. A chimney for a conventional flue has to be lined with lightweight stainless steel flexible tubing, for corrosive fumes will otherwise eventually rot brickwork.

A balanced or sealed-entry flue requires an opening in the outside wall to discharge fumes and take in fresh air. This has a duct and grill surround. You must not fix nearer than 300mm to a window or a door.

There are two variations on a microbore installation — the open system or the sealed system. In effect, all heating systems are "closed", but there may be a need to restore loss of water through evaporation or the expulsion of air from the system and the water.

As the system settles down, the "live" oxygenated air separates and has to be bled from the system. This is conventionally done by releasing air, via a bleed valve in a radiator at a high point in the system.

The open system utilises a feed-and-expansion cistern in

the loft which automatically tops up water loss. An expansion pipe has to be fitted to curve over the storage cistern to allow expansion hot-water to vent if necessary. In practice the make-up cistern should only rarely operate.

The sealed system gives greater versatility with the low water-content principle. This uses a pressure vessel to take up water expansion, and no make-up cistern is needed. This unit is mounted on or near the boiler and should be sized to the water content of the system. Manufacturers can supply the relevant advice.

With a sealed system you can operate at higher working temperatures than with an open system, so you can use a smaller boiler still and achieve even faster heat-up and recovery. This may mean, however, that the "touch" temperatures of conventional radiators are too high to be comfortable and you need to choose an enclosed pattern or use fan or natural convectors.

Venting of air is achieved by an automatic air vent. As sealed systems achieve a pressure of around two atmospheres (A), in use, also fit a pressure gauge. You can buy a unit combining a pressure-vessel gauge and air vent. You should also fit a pressure-release valve.

To operate a pumped-primary heating system, you require a cylinder thermostat, which operates one of the diverter valves or one "swing" of the three-port valve, with a room thermostat, which controls the heating temperature.

There is a wide range of controls you can choose from. You can link the system with a programmer, which enables you also to choose heating and hot-water cycles of operation. It is, however, worth considering a night set-back arrangement, where the heating operates continually and goes down to a predetermined lower level at night.

This means that there is far less heating energy needed the

next morning to recover lost heat — and you have an initially more comfortable home. If your home is well-insulated, a night set-back control will actually cut heating bills.

What are your heating needs? A small home may need less than 12.8 kW/h while a larger detached or "semi" may need 17.1 kW. A four-bedroomed home may need 20 kW or more.

Boiler ratings are given in kilowatts (kW) or BTU/h (British thermal units per hour). The BTU is being phased out gradually as a unit of heat measurement, since the kilowatt is a metric value and heat-loss calculations are now usually worked out to a metric formula.

Stale air will build up in the home, so despite the needs to conserve heat, you must have adequate ventilation. This more often than not, is taken care of naturally — by any small gaps around doors and windows, chimneys and the opening of outside doors.

The suggested comfort levels to aim at are:

Kitchen	16°C
Toilet, hall, cloakroom, staircase, bathroom	19°C
Living room, dining room	21°C
Bedroom	15°C

You can use a simple formula to work out your heat losses and determine heat requirements. Measure the room volume in m³ (cubic metres) and for a temperature of 21°C, multiply this by 83. For 15°C multiply by 63, and for 13°C by 49. This provides the figure in watts; to obtain kilowatts, divide by 1000.

Allow around 25 per cent extra boiler capacity to cope with exceptionally cold weather.

For conventional installations, the water content of a system is about 30 litres for every kilowatt of heat with radiators and around 15 litres per kW for skirting or fan convectors.

The amount of radiator surface can be arrived at from manufacturer's data. Skirting radiators emit 0.123kW/h per metre. Another rule-of-thumb method is to allow 2.60m of radiator surface for every 23.31 cubic metres of space. Allow 3.15 sq. metres for double radiators.

The distance from a manifold to a radiator or a convector should not exceed 7.5m, with a total combined flow-and-return pipework of more than 15m. For most purposes, 8mm tube can be used from manifolds. However, where a large radiator or convector is some distance away, it may function better with 10mm tube, while a small unit, fairly close to the manifold, may best be connected with 6mm tubing.

Microbore pipe comes on reels of various lengths and you simply unroll it. It is easily cut with a junior hacksaw. Remove any burrs from the cut end with a flat file and square off if necessary. Slightly round the outside of the pipe so that it enters the fitting easily. Push home and tighten up the compression lock-nut.

When running pipework parallel with joists, clip with pipe clips at intervals. Use a flat wood bit to bore holes through joists at a depth of 50mm.

Once you have obtained your "kit of parts", work closely to a plan. Work out your pipework runs and clear the working areas. Lift floorboards and put them back loosely.

Fit all radiators and connectors, connect up radiator pipework and put in manifolds and the "header" supply pipework. Fit the expansion cistern and related parts or the pressure vessel.

Run pipework for domestic hot water. Fit the boiler and flue.

Fit the gas supply or oil line and check that the main supply is adequate. You can also run gas-heating systems from replaceable butane supplies in areas where there is no mains gas service.

Connect up the primary circuit between the boiler and the hot-water cylinder and the pipework circuitry to the boiler.

At the lowest point in the circuit, fit a drain cock. These are known as MT fittings (it stands for empty). This is so that the system can be drained down and flushed out.

Check all connections carefully. You can use 15mm compression fittings, reduced down using reducing sets to the size required, or appropriate compression or capillary fittings.

Fill up, check for leaks, then fit thermostats and other electrical equipment, or mechanical controls where preferred. It is a good idea to flush out a new installation after a couple of weeks and recharge.

CERAMIC WALL TILING

Wall tiles are among the most durable of wall surfaces, look attractive, are easy to clean and maintain and simple to apply.

Ceramic tiles are produced in two main sizes — 108mm × 108mm and 152mm×152mm. When estimating for wall tiles, allow 86 of the small tiles or 44 of the large ones per square metre of wall. To the total, add 5 per cent for cutting, wastage and breakage.

There are also round edged (RE) tiles — some with one rounded edge and others with two — known as 1RE and 2RE respectively. Field tiles, which are glazed on one edge, but not rounded, are being increasingly introduced.

Tiles are fixed with tile adhesive, and there is a variety of suitable makes. Use a waterproof type where moisture is present, such as a shower room. There are also different adhesives for internal and external use.

Before tiling, make sure that all surfaces are firm, level and dry. Avoid tiling on new plaster. On a dusty surface, brush down and apply a surface sealant.

Most tiles have spacer lugs on the edges. This produces an even spacing which you fill with a white, compressible

7. Tiling datum point. Position batten one tile high and work from this. Wall and floor surfaces are seldom true.

powder called grouting, and makes a neat appearance. You mix this up to a creamy consistency with water.

You need the following tools: A notched adhesive spreader usually supplied with the adhesive, though you can buy a notched tiling trowel if you have a lot of tiling to do, pincers, to trim tiles, a carborundum tile cutter, a spirit level or a plumb-bob, a sponge or a tiler's squeegee, to apply grout to the tile joints, and a long batten.

The latter is used as a tiling datum point. You never tile from skirtings or flooring surfaces as these may not be true.

Adhesive is supplied in cans, ready mixed, or in a paste form which you mix to a creamy consistency with clean water. Do not mix more than you can use, for it cannot be reconstituted.

Temporarily nail-fix the batten along the wall, so you can remove it later, at the height of one tile up from the floor or skirting. Check that it is horizontal. Mark out the batten in tile widths so that you can space tiles to avoid awkward cuts and present a balanced look. You can adjust the spacing slightly if necessary. It is important that you maintain both horizontal and vertical alignment, for errors will show up.

Use the plumb-bob or a spirit level to mark vertical lines at the ends of each wall, spaced one tile in, and work to this as you tile. These two rows, the top tiles at ceiling level and the bottom row are put in after the main tiling and may have to be trimmed to fit.

Apply the adhesive thinly with the notched trowel over an area of about a square metre. The ridges formed by the notches give good suction to the tiles. If the adhesive is not applied evenly or the wall is untrue, some tiles will be proud of the surface.

Place, do not slide, the tiles in place. If the tiles do not possess spacer lugs, make these up from small pieces of card, which can be removed after the adhesive has dried.

Leave the tiles for several hours, then remove the batten and fill in the remaining tiles at bottom, top and sides. Trim these to fit. You lightly "butter" the backs of these individually using the small metal trowel. Use a similar technique

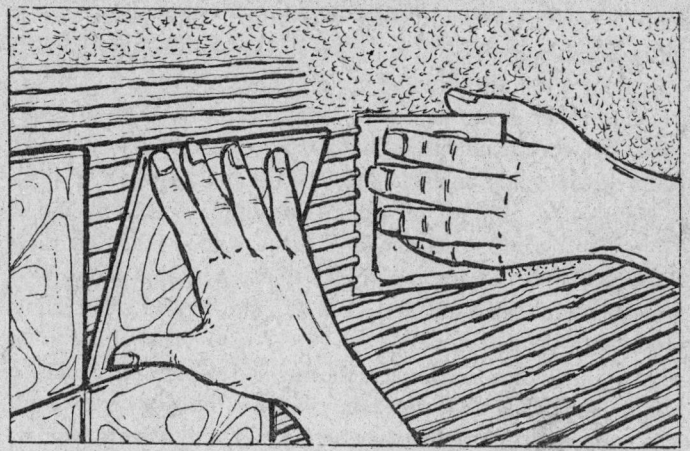

8. Placing tiles in position. Use a notched spreader to apply adhesive and place – never slide – the tiles into position.

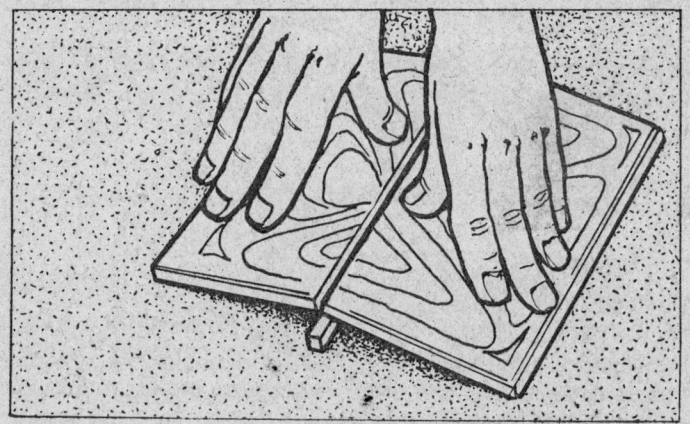

9. Cutting a tile. Break tile glaze with the tile cutter, then press down evenly over a match-stick or small batten to break cleanly.

with a batten above kitchen work tops, cupboards, sinks, baths and basins.

To cut a tile, use a metal straight edge to guide the cutter. Measure, then score across to break the glaze. Place a small sliver of wood, such as a match-stick, beneath the tile and press down evenly on each side. The tile should break evenly.

Pincers are used to "nibble" tiles to shape. Take only small "bites" at a time. You can drill a tile with a masonry or a glass drill bit, but for larger holes, use a radius tile cutter, which is adjustable for size. Drill at a slow speed when using a power drill.

Grout the joins to complete the finished effect after about 12 hours. Rub the paste firmly in the joins with the sponge or squeegee, and, when dry, polish the tiles clean. To improve the finish, run a slightly rounded piece of stick lightly across the joints.

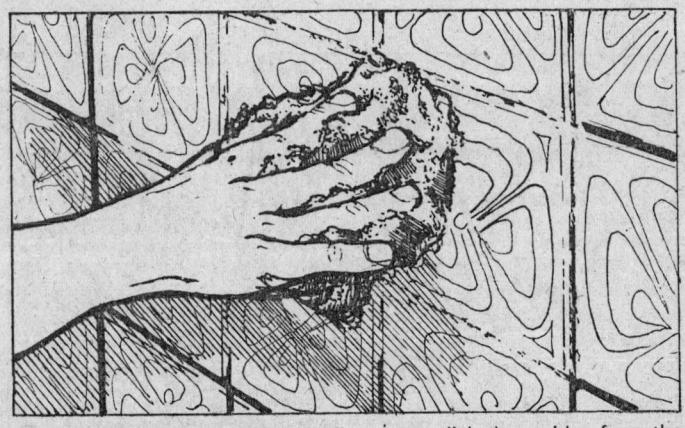

10. Grouting is used to fill the tile gaps; polish the residue from the tile face with a soft cloth.

Use glazed edge of RE (round-edged) tiles on the reveal side of a window and not the abutting main wall. When tiling above a reveal, the tiles will have to be propped in place with a long batten while setting.

Mosaic tiles, which may consist of a large square of tiles on a gauze backing, are fixed in the same manner as larger tiles. You can trim a square and also cut individual tiles.

CHIMNEYS

Chimney care should be part of a programme of regular roof maintenance. One of the first signs of trouble may be damp patches on the interior wall of the chimney breast. The most likely cause is damp, due to defective flashing or inadequate ventilation in the flue.

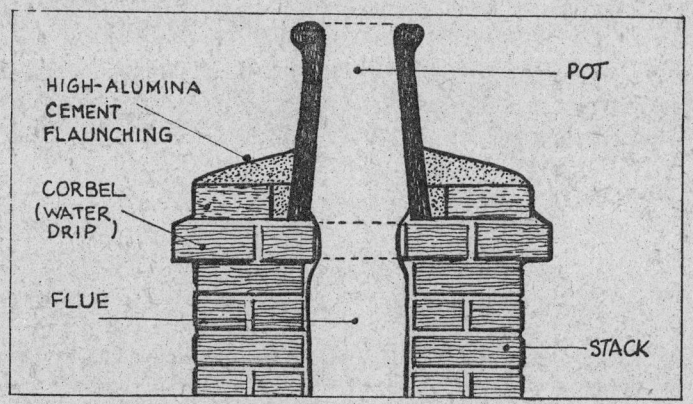

HIGH-ALUMINA CEMENT FLAUNCHING

CORBEL (WATER DRIP)

FLUE

POT

STACK

11. Chimneys. Arrangement of an average stack and chimney pot.

Always use the correct access equipment, for any roof work. See page 167.

Flashing is the weatherproof seal used where the chimney abuts the roof. In older homes this may consist of lead or zinc which deteriorate in time and become porous, or a mortar fillet, called haunching, which has cracked.

Alternatively the flaunching, the mortar fillet round the chimney pot, may have cracked or broken away, as a result of expansion and contraction near a heat source.

Repairing flashings

Rather than replace lead flashing, unless this is unavoidable, it may be easier to use one of the modern aluminium-based bituminous flashing materials or a mastic glazing tape. Instructions for use are provided by the manufacturers.

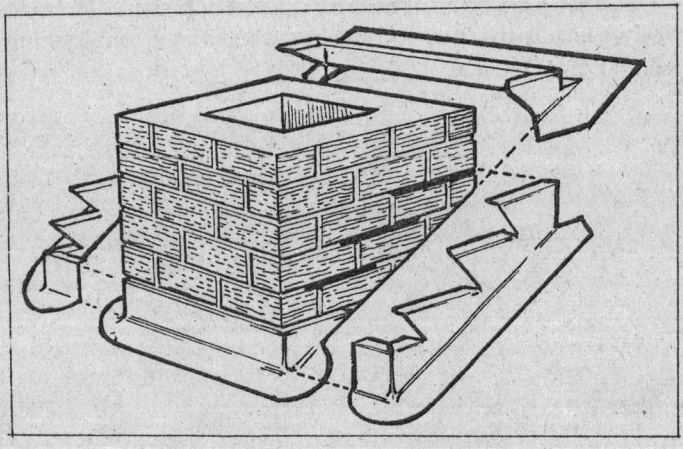

12. Stepped flashing. Chimney stacking showing stepped flashing at the side and apron flashing at the top and the bottom.

Use cold bitumen to repair slightly damaged flaunching. Badly damaged mortar must be removed and renewed with a 1:3 cement-mortar mix. Before applying the mortar, brush on a dilute PVA adhesive to bond the surface. Apply with a small steel trowel.

You can repair damaged haunching in the same way but use a plasterer's wooden float. Use a stiff mix and allow the first coat to dry, then cross-scratch the surface with the trowel tip to provide good adhesion for the finish coat. Trowel this smooth with a steel float.

A damaged chimney pot must be replaced. Block up the fireplace opening and secure the pot with a rope. Then chip away at the mortar with a club hammer and bolster. When the pot is free lower it to the ground.

Dampen round the inner edge of the surround and brush on a dilute PVA solution. Remortar with a mix of one part of high-alumina cement and three parts of soft sand. Position the new pot and adjust to sit vertically by inserting packing pieces of slivers of tile or slate. Take care that mortar does not fall down the flue.

If you block up a fireplace opening insert ventilation grills in the chimney breast to allow air circulation.

Another cause of damp may be a blockage caused by a bird's nest. This should be removed.

CLADDING

Wall cladding — solid timber, veneered plywood, melamine-faced surfacings on hardboard or plywood — makes an attractive home feature finish. Average sheet sizes for large panels are between 2.44m × 1.22m to 3.05m × 1.22m. Single planks are either square-edged or tongued and grooved. You can also clad ceilings.

Avoid cladding newly plastered surfaces. On damp areas, cover the surface with 500-gauge polythene or a metal-foil lining, or paint with a rubberised solution.

Cladding – sheets or individual planks – can be fixed to

13. Spacing of battens. Horizontal and vertical battens should be spaced evenly for fixing cladding to wall surfaces.

wall battens or, on clean, flat surfaces, stuck directly to the wall with contact adhesive. A rubberised gap-filling adhesive, applied from a special dispenser, can be used to stick cladding directly to walls that are slightly uneven.

Sheet cladding is available in a wide range of veneers and decorative finishes. Some are prefinished with varnish or ready for finishing. On wood-grained cladding, the sheets may be grooved to represent random planking. The long edges are usually bevelled to provide a groove where panels join.

Planks

Planking is made in a range of timbers and profiles and usually between 75mm and 150mm wide

Condition any cladding by bringing into the room to acclimatise to temperature and humidity for about 48 hours before fixing.

Fix battens with masonry nails or plug and screw-fix to walls. Fix horizontally and vertically at roughly 300mm centres or distances. The panel edges should meet in the centre of a vertical batten.

Cut panels or planking with an 8–10 point saw, or a power saw. Make sure you cut on a firm surface.

14. How to cut the cladding. Cut cladding on the face side with a sharp, fine-toothed saw at a shallow angle on a firm base.

Fix with 32mm pins or lost-head nails, where possible through the grooving, punch below the surface and fill with a stopping or bees-wax. You can trim openings for light fittings with a sharp handyman's knife.

Since ceilings are often irregular, you may have to scribe the tops of sheets so that they contour accurately. Cut the panels slightly over length and push these against the ceiling close to the wall. Take a small block of wood and run this along against the ceiling, holding a pencil beneath the block, so that the contour is transferred. Trim to this line.

On internal corners, butt panels together. External corners, unless you mitre the long edges with a plane, are best butted to a matching vertical timber fillet.

15. Nailing the planks. "Secret" method of nailing planks through the tongues.

16. Cramping. Cramping timber matching using a scrap block of wood together with an old chisel.

Start cladding with planking from one corner; check the first strip with a spirit level to ensure this is vertical, for this is your reference or datum point. If this is tongued and grooved, saw off the tongue. You may have to scribe vertically, for walls are often untrue.

Pin the first board through the face. Fix all planks by "secret" nailing into the grooves at an angle. The next tongue covers this and any slight damage when fixing is concealed.

Leave a 6mm gap at top and bottom for ventilation.

Cramp the planks tightly against each other in turn with an old chisel, levered against the batten. You cannot cramp the last two. Fit these loosely — they will be slightly bowed — and then give them a blow with the fist to push them home. Nail through the face of the grooves.

Internal corners need no special treatment — just butt the edges of two planks. On external corners, cut off the groove from one length, to square the edge. Glue and pin this and repeat for the abutting plank. Treat the exposed edges with a wood dye.

CONDENSATION

Condensation can cause both structural and surface damage to your home. Air always contains water vapour which is taken up as it heats. If the temperature drops or the air comes into contact with a cold surface the water condenses — returns to its liquid state.

The warmer the air the more water is retained as vapour. Saturation occurs when the air can hold no more water — the temperature at which this happens is known as the "dew point"

The main causes are poor ventilation, the low internal temperature of walls, ceilings, windows and other cold surfaces and the amount of water vapour in the air in the home.

Condensation problems are most likely in bathrooms and kitchens, where steam is present. You can use louvre windows, open a small window or install simple plastic window grills. These are activated by air pressure. Alternatively, an extractor fan, wall or window mounted, will help to pull steam out of the home. Site these as high and as near the source of steam as possible.

When using steam-producing appliances, such as washing machines and tumble dryers or cooking close the door where these are in use.

When you run a bath run a small amount of cold water before adding the hot. This will cut the steam build-up. Paraffin-burning appliances give off large quantities of moisture.

A combination of controlled heating and common sense, in terms of ventilation, will give a better living environment and help to cut condensation which can cause discomfort to you and deterioration of your decorative surfaces and furnishings

DAMP

One of the most persistent problems, particularly in older homes, is that of damp, and one of the most common causes is either that the house has no damp-proof course (DPC) or that this has broken down. This means that there is no barrier to prevent water rising, through capillary action, from the ground and being absorbed into the brickwork and plaster.

One of the first signs may be a band of staining, usually just above the skirting board, or peeling paper and an unpleasant, musty smell. Unseen, joists and floorboards may quickly become affected by wet or dry rot.

Silicone injection

17. Drilling injection holes. Injection holes are drilled at intervals in brickwork of solid walls for silicone treatment of damp.

The solution is to renew, repair or provide a damp-proof course, which should be about 150mm above ground level. There are various methods.

Cutting out

This involves using a chain saw to cut out one section of brickwork at a time and inserting a layer of bituminous felt or slates, encased between layers of waterproof concrete. Alternatively, you can insert a DPC of hard engineering bricks which you mortar into place, a section at a time, and then make good. This however is quite a skilled job and may be better left to a specialist.

18. Injecting silicon fluid. Bottles containing silicone fluid are inserted, and when the wall will accept no more liquid, the damp course is complete.

Silicone injection

This is an injected system for use where it is not practical to insert a conventional DPC. Drill holes in the wall internally and externally at intervals of 250mm at an angle of 45° and inject silicone fluid. You can buy or hire bottles from specialist firms such as Richardson & Starling. The job is complete when the brickwork will not accept any more liquid.

Electro-osmosis

Electro-osmosis is a specialist job but may be the only answer if your walls are very thick or the party-wall DPC has failed. Ribbons of copper or copper wiring are inserted into the walls at DPC level and these are connected to copper earth rods set into the soil.

The principle on which this works is that as an electrical charge exists associated with the moisture rise between the

19. An air brick. Keep air bricks free, so that air can circulate beneath floorboards and prevent wood rot.

wall and the earth, the careful positioning of the copper in the wall and the earth rods creates a low-resistance circuit between the soil and the building.

The electricity is discharged to earth and the dampness can no longer rise above this charge. This is carried out by specialists such as Rentokil Ltd.

Damp patches may occur for other reasons. One of the most common is that soil has been allowed to pile up against external walls, above the DPC, rendering it ineffective. The simple solution is to move the débris and keep it clear.

Another cause may be a brick tie in a cavity wall, originally left encrusted with mortar, providing a dampness bridge between the outer and inner skins. The only remedy is to cut out the brickwork and clean up the tie.

Floors

At one time, floors were often laid directly on to bare earth. If this type of floor starts to give trouble you may be able to treat this with a coat of damp-inhibiting epoxy-pitch resin, but if this fails it will be necessary to take up the floor and put down a damp-proof membrane. This may be liquid bitumen, which is poured on to the floor and spread evenly, or 500-gauge sheet polythene.

In both cases, make sure that the membrane reaches at least 150mm up the walls and cut the polythene into the DPC course or the brickwork.

DÉCOR AND DESIGN

Home décor is very much a question of individual pre-ference, but thoughtful use of colour, space and pattern can help to create a balanced living environment and disguise design features of your home that are a visual problem.

Each area in the home should achieve unity, look attrac-tive and yet be practical for the activity that goes on in it.

Colour is a very important aspect of any décor scheme. Over two thousand colours can be achieved by blending the primary colours, red, blue and green. Black and grey and white are non-colours, but can be used as foils for colour schemes, based on variations of the primary colours.

Rooms facing north will feel warmer and sunnier if decorated in the red, red-orange, yellow range, the warmer colours of the spectrum. Use red sparingly, particularly in small areas where it can give a closed-in, over-stimulating effect.

Colours in the cool spectrum can be used to advantage in south-facing rooms or to give a feeling of space.

Otherwise-attractive rooms may be out of proportion. Colour can help give balance. If a room is too wide for its length, use light colours on far walls and a warmer or darker colour on short walls to bring these in and reduce the feeling of width. Reverse this process for a long, narrow room.

If an area has too many doors, "lose" these to the eye by painting them in the same colour as the wall surface, or you can paper them. Paint radiators to match the background colour.

Striped floor coverings are usually laid with the stripe

towards the far end of the room, seen from the door. This will appear to lengthen a short room and laid widthways, widen a narrow area.

Too-high ceilings often spoil an otherwise attractive area. These can be lowered by fitting a false ceiling, such as illuminated ceiling panelling, or wood cladding fixed to a frame.

Alternatively, you might paint the ceiling and the top part of the wall in a dark colour to detract from its height and bring the eye focus down.

In a small room, avoid highly textured and brightly patterned wall and flooring surfaces. Certainly have no more than one patterned area. Choose restful colours such as gold, beige, soft greens and browns, perhaps highlighting focal points with a primary colour interest.

Self furnishings

A feeling of spaciousness is given by close carpeting adjoining rooms in the same colour if not the same quality so that open doors give a feeling of endless vista.

In a large room, close carpeting will only increase the feeling of size. Large areas can take pattern but not too many conflicting designs. Use either a pattern carpet or a large textured and patterned central rug as a point of focus and keep the carpet surround dark.

Blinds take up less space then curtains in a small room, and can also provide camouflage for an unattractive view or provide a focal point.

It is easy to overfurnish a room. Try to see space as activity areas and group the furniture accordingly and use space in your layout. For example, a large living area may have furniture grouped for both relaxation and dining areas. These may be visually linked by the colours of wall and floor surfaces, or divided by changing these from one area to another.

If lack of height in an area is a problem, striped wall-covering that draws the eye upwards will help; use a floor covering to tone in with the wall surface covering. Floor-length curtains and tall furniture tend to give a feeling of height, while low-level furniture brings the centre of focus down.

In a small room, modular, wall-hung storage units will increase the feeling of space, leaving the floor area free.

Dark walls and surfaces will not necessarily make a small area seem smaller if they are well contrasted with plenty of white on the ceiling and woodwork. This type of colour scheme may be best in a south-facing room.

Where the space is small, an illusion of vista can be given by using mirrors skilfully. Hallways, small bathrooms, in fact, any area in the home will benefit where a double vista can be made to deceive the eye. An added bonus is that mirrors reflect more light into the home.

DOUBLE GLAZING

Double glazing is an important part of whole-home insulation but while adding to comfort levels, eliminating cold zones and cutting condensation it will not save vastly on your fuel bills. Double glazing can also help to assist sound insulation.

Up to 20 per cent of all heat loss is via window areas. Double glazing works on the principle that two sheets of glass, with a sandwich of air between them act as a better insulator than a single pane of glass. The wider the gap the better the insulation.

The simplest, but probably the most expensive way to double glaze, is to use pre-sealed factory-made units. These are two sheets of glass with a filling of inert gas. In place they look just like single glazing. You have no summer storage problems – only two sides to clean and no condensation.

Units can be custom built but as they are twice as heavy as single sheets of glass you will have to check that your existing frames are sound and strong enough to support them. Most sealed units have a 5mm air space and you will need a 12mm window rebate, at least, to fix these in a wood

20. Double-glazing – applied sash

or metal frame. Some units are available for smaller rebates. Check the size you will require and take all measurements, for units, very carefully before you order.

Fix with beading or set the units into non-hardening compound. To double-glaze existing windows, you add a second panel of glass. There is a variety of methods collectively called coupled sashes, or secondary window systems.

Applied sashes are fixed to an existing window frame, and provide a second layer of glass that insulates yet can be removed for storage and cleaning.

Sliding-sash units fit into the surround framework and allow, for example, two-double-glaze sections to slide one behind the other and give access to the outer window.

This type of sash consists of head and sill track and side members. Position the head track to allow space for projecting window furniture. Sliding-sash units can be fitted even if the window frame is out of true as most manufacturers supply packing pieces to correct this.

The hinged unit is the third type of secondary window; an inner window, which you can open for cleaning and ventilation, and usually consists of a coupled sash. Most coupled sashes have aluminium framework, though it is possible to buy kits to make up yourself. These usually have PVC framing. Manufactured units can usually be on a supply-and-fix basis or supplied ready for you to fix.

When you fit any secondary window make sure that you choose the correct weight of glass for the window area. For general purposes 4mm thick glass is adequate.

You can make up your own fixed applied-sash units by fixing a second pane to the window frame but condensation will tend to form inside the glass. To minimise this either use silica-gell crystals placed along the bottom of the frame, to absorb the moisture — but these need to be dried out

21. Sliding sash, which gives access to main windows.

22. Opening sash, which also gives access to main windows.

periodically — or drill small holes upwards, in the base of the frame, to provide ventilation.

As the heat between the two windows will draw out any moisture in the timber it is a good idea to seal the reveal with adhesive-backed aluminium foil.

There is a wide range of kits on the market which you can make up using clear glass. One type, produced by Lumite Ltd, however, uses self-adhesive channelling and clear acrylic sheeting.

The Polycell system claims to offer the only double-glazing kits for sliding-sash windows.

DRAINS

Waste systems do not usually need a great deal of attention but regular inspection of waste traps, gullies and manholes (correctly called inspection chambers) is always advisable.

Grease and débris can build up to cause blockage. A grating should always be fitted over the gulley. This should be scrubbed periodically with a wire brush and a solution of hot water, soda and disinfectant.

If a blockage occurs in the manhole inspection chamber, the fault may be cleared by prodding the obstruction free with a piece of wood. For major blockages, you need a set of drainage rods and fittings. These can usually be hired, or you can buy.

Rods are around 1m long, and screw together to the length required. There are various attachments for dealing with differing obstructions. These include a scraper, a corkscrew attachment, a hook and a rubber plunger.

Twist the assembled rods in a clockwise direction when in use. This ensures that they do not unscrew. Once you have freed the blockage and removed débris, scrape all surfaces clear and flush out with clean water.

A possible cause of build up of débris and subsequent blockage are fractures, causing waste to adhere and rough benching — the interior sloping manhole sides. This should be smooth and slope gently.

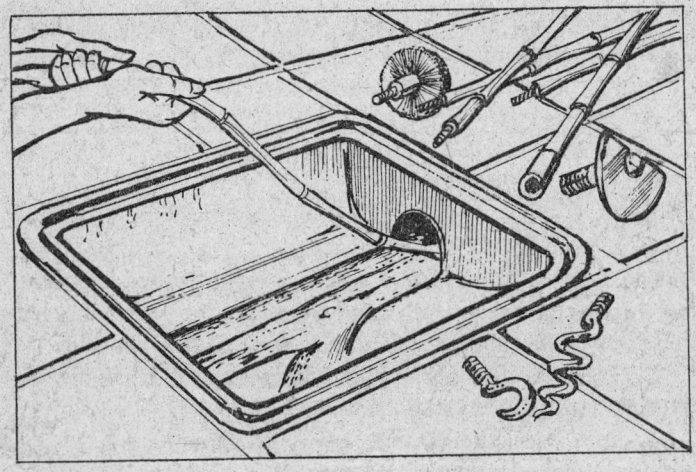

23. An inspection chamber, together with a set of rods and various attachments.

To make good any damage, clean the surface thoroughly, brush on PVA solution, a liquid adhesive, and repair, using a mixture of one part of cement to three parts of sharp sand. Smooth with a steel trowel; allow the repair to dry thoroughly. Use a "prompt" (quick-drying) cement if the repair is urgent.

To test a manhole or a suspect length of drainage, you need drain plugs, which screw into the drainage pipe and expand to close it. A fall of more than 25mm in an hour in a manhole suggests leakage, not loss accountable for by natural evaporation. To release the water afterwards, in a controlled way, you unscrew a centre plug.

Damaged manhole covers should be discarded. The cover comes complete with its own manhole ring, so replace as a pair, mortaring in the new ring. Grease the inside lip of the ring to make an airtight seal.

ELECTRICITY

Old and out-of-date electrics can be dangerous and certainly neither sufficiently versatile nor adequate for present-day use and the demands of modern appliances.

Today, electrical materials are vastly improved and represent the many advances made in recent years. Old wiring may become perished and dangerous after a period of more than 25 years; it will certainly be inadequate for modern needs.

Rewiring a house can take time and be very disruptive. There is need for access beneath flooring and in the loft. With old wiring, the fuse box usually matches this in antiquity.

This section is intended to provide general guidelines on how to go about replacing outdated wiring and deal with electrical faults. If in doubt, always get experienced advice; and never do anything electrically without disconnecting the supply and being absolutely sure of what you are doing.

Modern lighting cables are PVC-encased and have an indefinite life, unlike the old rubber-sheathed ones which perish in time. These now follow a metric standard but are perfectly satisfactory to connect to older imperial PVC-clad cable.

Detailed domestic electrical rewiring needs careful planning. Clear rooms one at a time as you work and ensure that you are not left without light or power at any stage.

Ring mains

Modern power circuitry utilises a ring main — the three wires, live, neutral and earth — are connected together in a continuous ring to 13A sockets, which accept plugs with three square pins. Plugs contain individual fuses which should match the A (ampère) rating of the appliance. Sockets can be switched or unswitched without affecting the operation of the ring circuit.

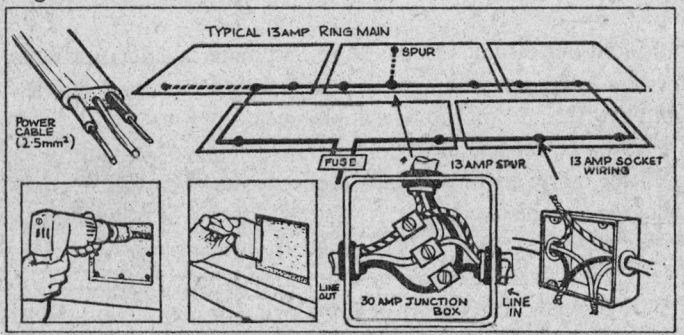

24. A ring-main. Arrangement of a ring-main circuit, and stages of fitting a plaster-depth metal box.

The ring main spreads the electrical load evenly over the entire circuit. You can run spur points — separate fused outlets — from the ring main. You can fit two to each spur, but the total number of spur outlets must not exceed the total number of ring-main outlets.

All socket outlets must be fitted in earthed metal boxes. Sockets can be flush or surface-mounted. Ensure that you provide a sufficient number of overall outlets for this avoids trailing flexes. A good, general spacing is a single or double socket at intervals of roughly two metres.

An average number of outlets is: kitchen, four; living area, three; dining area, two; bedrooms, two; hall and landing, one each. Garage points can be linked to the ring mains. In practice, however, it may be simpler to provide a separate radial circuit.

Older power wiring is generally in the form of a radial circuit which connects every appliance by an individual set of wires back to the fuse box.

When carrying out a full electrical rewiring, it is a good idea to consider separate up- and downstairs ring mains and lighting circuits, so that different areas can be isolated. For an area of greater than 300 sq. metres, you need to have two ring mains.

Water heaters and similar high-wattage appliances should be provided with separate circuits. For different reasons, a freezer should also be on a separate circuit, with the switch out of the reach of children. A cooker must always be on a separate circuit because of the high wattage.

When running cables beneath floorboards, clear the room, turn off power and lever up the flooring to expose a working area. You can cut floorboards across joists with a power saw, or use a special floorboard handsaw, then lever up the boards with a crowbar or a case opener. Take care not to cut through or disturb the existing cables.

If the cable has to run at right angles to joists, bore holes through the joists, using a power drill and wood flat bit, at a minimum depth of 50 mm. Do not cut notches to recess the cables; it is all too easy to nail or screw through into these afterwards. Where cables run parallel with the joists, fix these, at intervals, to the joists with cable clips.

Because floorboards may be fixed under skirtings, it may not be easy to lift boards near the position of your power point. In this case, drill a hole and "fish" for the cable with a loop of wire and pull it through. Feed the next section of cable through the hole to the next point. Allow sufficient wire so that you can bare and trim the wires and finally connect.

On each radial circuit, you can fit six single and one double socket or two spurs for a room of 30 sq. metres, and use a 20A main fuse.

With a solid ground floor, the cable must be fed through the wall inside conduiting. You will need to channel out and make good after inserting the conduit. Another possibility is to use plastic skirting conduiting, which replaces conventional skirting boards, to contain the cable.

Cables buried in walls, for lighting or power, must be run in either plastic or metal conduiting. This prevents them from accidental damage, and also enables the cables to be pulled through in the event of fault.

Lighting
Old lighting wiring and fitments can be lethal. Frayed flexes and worn switches are dangerous. It is illegal to use wall switches in bathrooms.

When replacing worn flexes or fitments, always make sure that the power is off and the fuses removed or switched out for added safety.

Modern lighting circuitry can be connected via either plate connections on some types of ceiling rose, taken in turn to feed other light fittings, called the "loop-in" method, or connected to a series of junction boxes, linked, in turn, to ceiling roses

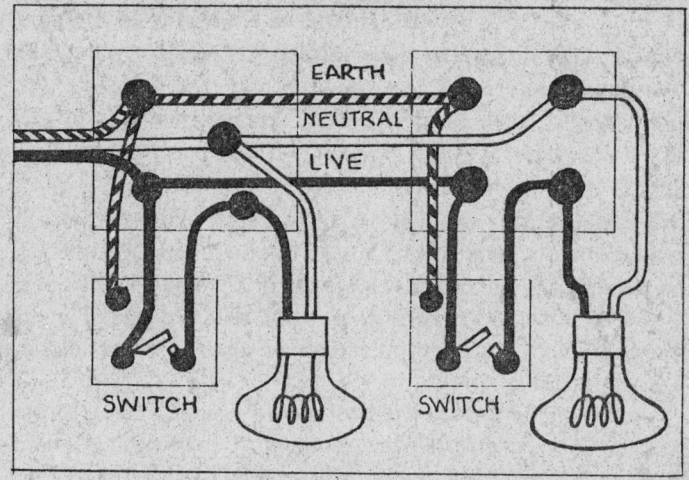

25. Lighting circuit. How to wire up a lighting circuit.

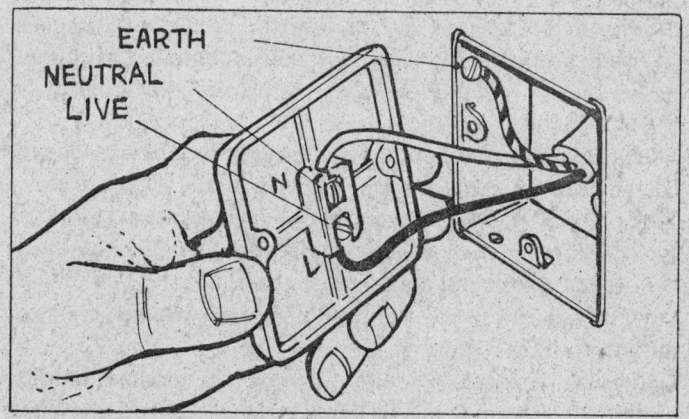

26. A switch. Connections for a standard light switch.

The live side of the switch should be connected to the light switch and returned to the live plate or connection on the rose or junction box. When you switch on, this completes the light circuit.

Safety

In a bathroom it is obligatory to fit a pull switch. Any wall switch must be located outside the door. Ceiling light fittings must be of a safe, enclosed pattern, or the lamp holder of a "skirted" type. No power point may be fitted in the bathroom, though a shaver point can be used if of a double-wound pattern.

In the kitchen, power points should not be nearer to the sink than one metre. Never mount a kitchen switch where you can inadvertently touch it with wet hands.

Fuses and connections

An old fuse box often sprouts into an arrangement of sub-boxes, not always safe and, at the best, crude. Replace any such arrangement with a new consumer unit, the modern name for a fuse box, or a miniature circuit breaker, or MCB.

The consumer unit contains a series of fuse blocks, one for each circuit fused to the rating of each circuit. The fuse blows to protect the circuit in the event of fault or overload. Some types of fuse block have individual switches.

The MCB does not contain fuses as such. Any fault causes the faulty circuit to switch off. It cannot be switched on again until the fault is rectified.

Provide separate circuits for ring mains and lighting circuits, garage power and lighting, front and side porches, freezer, cooker and water-heaters. There are colour codes on the front of the fuse blocks of some units to give a quick identification of the circuit. These are white (lighting), yellow (water heater), blue (power), red (ring mains), green (cooker).

Appliance fuses are of a cartridge type. Use 5A for lighting, 15A for water heaters, 30A for power, including ring mains, and 60A for cookers.

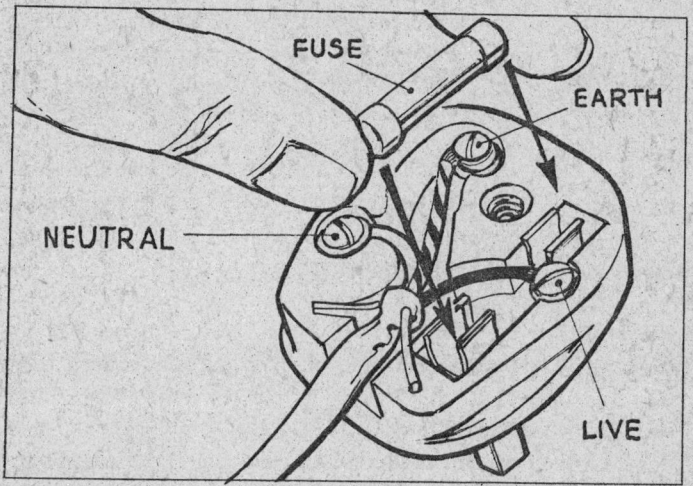

27. A fused plug. Connections for a plug. Use a fuse of the correct rating (A).

There are two categories of electrical wiring — flexible and fixed. Fixed wiring uses three conductors coloured red (live, or line), black (neutral), and unsheathed (earth). Flexible wiring has a brown (live) wire, blue (neutral) and green-and-yellow striped wire (earth). Cable ratings are determined by their cross-section area. The greater this is the higher the ampere rating.

This chart shows the types of cable and where it is used.

Cable (mm²)	Rating (A)	Use
1.0	11	*lighting flex*
1.5	13	*lighting and small power radial circuits*
2.5	18	*ring mains*
4.0	24	*individual power circuits*
6.0	31	*cookers*
10.0	42	*cookers*
16.0	56	*cookers dependent on wattage*

Strip back enough cable to connect to the terminal – no more. Twist each set of wires tightly together and tighten any screw in an anti-clockwise direction. Tighten any cable clamp so that the wire remains in place.

Fuse repairs
When a fuse blows, clean the blocked carbon deposit from the fuse carrier, for this sets up a high resistance which may cause the new fuse to melt.

Once your wiring is complete, the local electricity board will connect up to its own fuse box – provided your work is satisfactory! You have to provide two "tails" of heavy-duty cable for connection.

EXTERIOR CEMENT-RENDERED FINISHES

A bright new face on exterior brickwork can transform the appearance of the home. Where brickwork is sound, dry and clean, finishes, such as stone cement or nylon-bonded emulsion paints, offer good water-resistant surfaces. However, the surface remains only as good as the wall beneath, so brush this down well and make sure it is sound.

You can paint an existing cement finish with any of these paints, but make good any surface damage or cracks before doing so. Rub down the area with a stiff brush, and clean out cracks with the point of a trowel, undercut slightly, apply PVA liquid, then fill with new mortar.

The main exterior cement finishes are cement fining, shingle or pebble dash and roughcast. A hand-cranked machine can be used to apply a stippled finish – available in various colours – called Tyrolean. Another finish, called Ashlar, is basically cement fining, a slightly roughened cement finish, ruled out to represent blockwork.

A few tools are needed – a good-quality metal laying-on or finishing trowel, a pine skimming or wood float, a large water brush, to damp down wall areas to aid keying, a rubber or plastic bucket and a "devil" or scratcher to key-scratch the sub-surfaces.

Also needed is a wood floating rule – a piece of long straight-edged timber. This is used with screed rules – temporary battens – to level the surface across.

The skimming float can be used for finishing. It produces a slightly roughened surface. This float can also be adapted as a scratcher by knocking nails through the back. Tap these proud of the face when using as a devil float. You also need a large "spot" board for mixing.

Protect paths before beginning work.

Check all rendered surfaces by tapping. If the surface sounds hollow, the rendering has probably "blown" away from the wall, and must be removed. Use a club hammer and a bolster to remove affected areas.

Mix materials dry and add water sparingly. Mix to the consistency of thickened custard.

The render coat consists of one part of Portland cement to six parts of soft sand, with a small amount of mortar plasticiser. You may need to apply two thin coats.

A repair patch for a rendered surface consists of a mix of one part of Portland cement to one of soft (builder's sand, plus half a measure of lime, applied to the surface with a steel trowel. The final finish depends on whether it is shingle dash, rough cast, or cement fining.

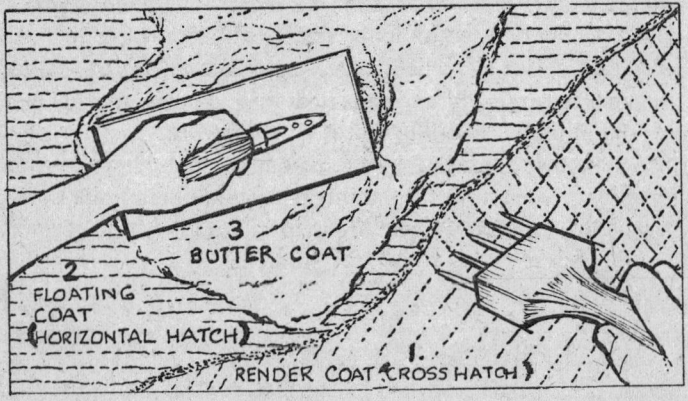

28. Key-hatching. Use a scratcher to key-hatch the surface of each coat as shown.

The floating coat consists of one part of cement to three parts of sand, and again it may be best to apply two thin coats. The butter coat consists of half a part of sand to three of cement, and a small quantity of lime. The latter aids suction.

Fix temporary vertical battens at distances of about 1850mm, and work between these.

Lay the render coat on with a steel trowel, using upward strokes and the full length of the trowel to "lay off". Level across between battens with the rule. Scratch the coat cross diagonally and leave for about 12 hours. Flatten out the burrs with the skimming float.

Apply the floating coat in a similar fashion, but scratch horizontally. The butter coat is only used when applying shingle dash and is applied to the floating coat after a further 12 hours.

Pea shingle should be clean, even and well washed. Put down polythene to pick up the shingle for reuse. Put it in a plastic bucket and flick it on to the butter coat with the back of the steel trowel. Do this evenly to avoid "bunching".

29. Exterior finishes. (Left) The three basic coats for exterior finishes. (Right) Shingle is flicked on to the butter coat.

Tap the shingle lightly with the skimming float to firm it. Wipe the face of the float frequently to keep it clean.

Roughcast incorporates pea shingle in a mix of $\frac{1}{2}$ part of cement to one part of lime, prepared to a sloppy consistency. This is flicked on to the floating coat. Apply from a bucket with the back of the laying-on trowel. Shingle dash can be left unpainted but roughcast requires a decorative paint finish.

Cement fining is applied to a floating coat. Wash the sand to remove any clay which can cause surface crazing. Mix one part of Portland cement to two parts of sand. Apply with the steel finishing trowel and rub over with the skimming float. Finish off with a sponge used with light, circular movements.

A variation on this is stipple finish. Finish as before and then stipple carefully over the surface with a stipple brush.

The Tyrolean finish, sometimes called "spatter-dash" is applied from a machine which you hire. You buy the special mixture, add water and load into the machine. As you crank a handle, the material is spattered in blobs on to the surface.

You can adjust the machine to vary the size of the blobs. Keep it moving to avoid a build-up in any area.

EXTRACTOR FANS AND AIR CLEANERS

Stale air, cooking odours and steam in the home are unpleasant – but the answer is not necessarily to open a window. Kitchens and bathrooms present particular ventilation problems, and in both there can be a build up of steam.

In an enclosed bathroom, with no windows, you must, by law, have a vented extraction system. These normally work on a fixed cycle and are activated when the light is switched on.

Elsewhere, ventilation normally occurs through windows, up chimney flues and through gaps in window frames. Cold air enters at the lowest level, heats, and escapes through higher-level openings.

In making homes thermally efficient, it is possible to create further problems of stale air and unwanted steam. For comfort, a minimum number of air changes are needed per hour.

These are the desirable number of air changes needed in average conditions:

Kitchen	*10–15 per hour*
Bathroom, WC	*10–15 per hour*
Living areas	*4–6 per hour*

The simplest ventilator is the window-mounted plastic grill which revolves as a result of the difference in air pressure between the inner and outer walls of the house.

Wall or window-mounted extractor fans

When using an electric wall- or window-mounted fan, make sure it is large enough for the cubic capacity of the room. Two or more fans may be needed in a very large area. Full fitting instructions are included with extractor fans.

A fan should be fitted as high up as possible and close to the source of steam or odour. Also, place as far as possible away from the main source of air replacement, usually the door. If you have a room-ventilated boiler or open fire, allow for adequate air replacement for the extractor *and* the heating unit.

Cooking smells and steam can be reduced or eliminated by installing a cooker hood. There are two main types: either a cooker hood connected to a ducting system which is fan-assisted, or a hood, hung over the cooker and wired in electrically which incorporates a fan and renewable charcoal filter pads to absorb the smells.

Air filters not only make the air smell pleasant but they also remove the minute particles of air-borne dust that can damage health. Units can be portable or fixed. These work on the principle of electrostatic precipitation.

A filter is electrically energised and the dirty air passes through an ionisation grid which gives the particles an electrical charge. It then passess over the collector plates –

one set positively and the other negatively charged. The charged particles are impelled towards the negative plates. The filter can be removed and periodically washed to remove the particles.

This type of unit has the advantage of being quiet in operation and does not remove your expensive warm air but merely cleans it.

FENCES

Wooden fences tend to rot because the posts have not been treated with creosote or other preservative or the base or gravel board has been covered with earth. Water rises and soon the whole fence deteriorates.

Concrete posts or spurs solve the problem of rotting posts. A rotted post, if not too damaged, can be cut and bolted to a spur.

Dig earth away from gravel boards and replace any that have rotted. Fix the board to short battens nailed to the post.

When replacing a post, try to remove this in one piece. If embedded in concrete, use a crowbar to lever it out.

If the slots for the arris rails are ready cut, it is a simple matter to reinsert the new post and tap these in. If you have to cut new slots or mortice, use the old post as a guide and mark out using a woodworking try-square, drill a line of holes with an auger bit and a hand brace, then chop out squarely with a chisel.

Soak the new post in preservative for 24 hours, and make sure that the mortice slots are thoroughly treated. Locate the post in the arris-rail ends, or mortices — you should have sufficient play to do this. Check with a spirit level that the

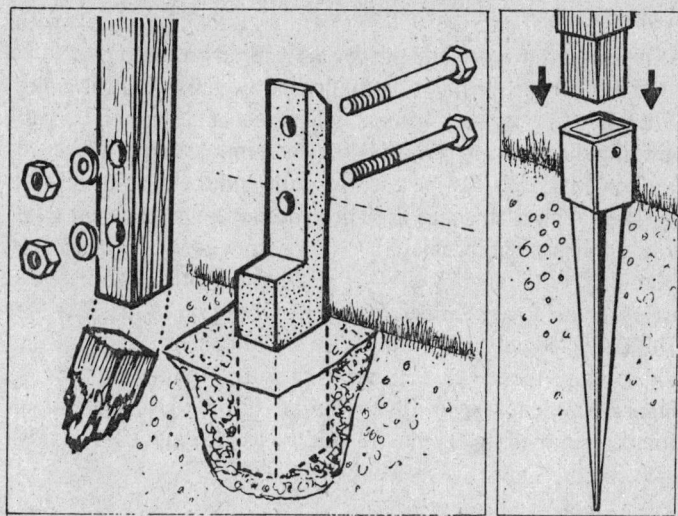

30. Two methods of replacing a damaged post. A concrete post
and a galvanised spike into which the trimmed post slots and is
screw fixed.

31. Fences need not rot! Keep gravel boards free of earth to prevent it.

post is vertical and the rails horizontal. Back fill the hole with concrete or hardcore and earth and ram down tightly.

Fix the rails firmly to the post by drilling dowel holes through the post and inserting a piece of dowel of corresponding diameter. Alternatively, use aluminium nails.

New arris rails can be cut to length and the ends or tenons trimmed with a chisel to fit. These do not have to be cut with a high degree of precision. Where an end of arris rail is damaged, you can saw this off and repair with a proprietary arris-rail strip, which fits over it and screws on to the post.

Feather-edged boards tend to rot at the top and bottom where damp penetrates. When replacing a board or boards, ensure that each overlap by about 12mm. Use an end of board, trimmed to 12mm in width, as a template for this.

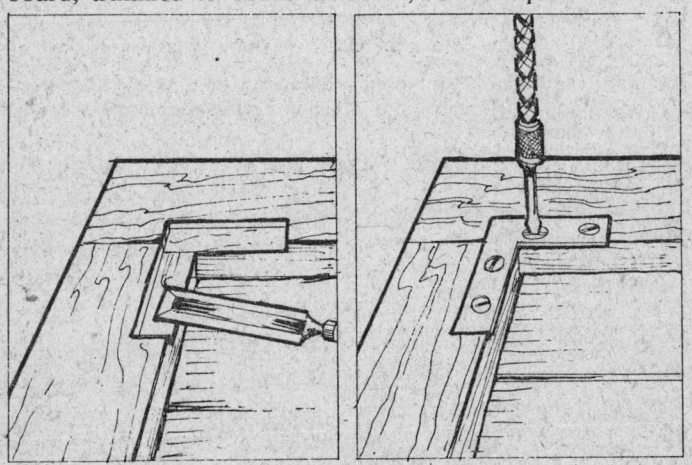

32. Doubtful joints on a gate. How to strengthen them.

Line up at top and bottom with the template held against the board as you nail. Check levels at around every fourth or fifth board.

To keep fences in good order, inspect regularly and treat with preservative. Keep earth from piling up against gravel boards.

A rotted gate may be difficult to repair and may be easier to replace. You can take a gate apart, if not in too advanced a stage of disrepair. Clean up joints and reglue and re-assemble, replacing any damaged sections. Doubtful joints can be reinforced by screwing on corner angle brackets, as in Fig. 32.

FIREPLACES

Fireplaces and chimney breasts are areas which may call for different orders of attention.

You may replace or refurbish a fireplace, to make it a focal point of attention, or brick it up.

When fitting a new fireplace surround, you may want to modify the grate for a solid-fuel or gas fire, both perhaps with back boiler, as part of a heating system, or repair or replace a damaged fireback.

A cracked fireback can be repaired with fireclay cement, sold in tins. Brush off soot and clean up. Slightly enlarge the crack and undercut it, using the tip of a small trowel, soak the fireback with water as this helps the fireclay to adhere. Trowel the cement into the crack and smooth off.

If you have to replace a damaged fireback, chip away the surrounding mortar with a club hammer and cold chisel. The old fireback should come out easily.

A new fireback will be supplied as a single unit; this needs separating into a top and lower half. Do this carefully by chipping around both sides with a sharp bolster and a club hammer.

Fit the lower half centrally, then trowel a weak (1:9:1) mortar mix (1 part cement, 9 parts sand, 1 part of lime) behind the lower section. Use a spirit level to check that the horizontal level is true.

Position the top half and trowel the weak mortar mix firmly behind. Prepare a mix of 1 part of cement to 4 parts of sand and slope a mortar fillet between the edges of the fireback and the chimney brickwork.

Between the top and bottom sections, moisten the joint and trowel in fireclay.

A fireplace fixes to the wall by edge plates, which are screwed into the wall beneath the plaster. It is only necessary to chip this away to unscrew and then remove the fireplace.

The old fireplace may include a hearthpiece. This will be heavy, so get help to lift it. Once the fireplace is removed, the hearth can be levered out with a case-opener.

Clean up the area of the new hearth, put down an even 1:4 (1 part of cement, four parts of sand) bed of mortar, then locate and joggle the new hearth into position.

Mark the fixings of the new fireplace on the wall and screw-fix, plugging the wall to ensure that these are firm.

You may wish to open up a chimney breast — or to fill it in. Before removing the face of the chimney, you will have to cut a slot and fit a lintel or a chimney bar. Bed the bar or the lintel in mortar before cutting the opening below.

It may be inadvisable to remove the "cheeks" of the chimney breast because this may support a fireplace above. You may need to remove the entire chimney structure and make good if you plan to demolish a complete fireplace in one room.

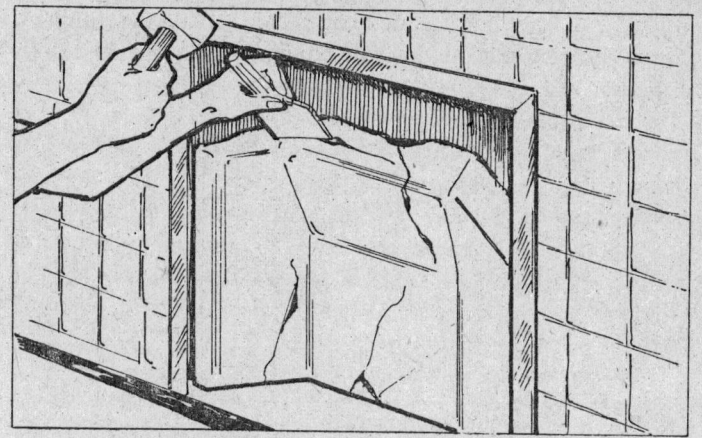

33. Chip out an old fireback with a club hammer and a cold chisel.

34. Mortar in the new fireback in two halves.

If you fill in the chimney breast, the infill brickwork must be cut in to the surrounding chimney brickwork. With ordinary bricks, cut out every third brick from the fireplace opening to bond in the brickwork. This is called "toothing". Similarly, you can fill in with building blocks; this will be

35. Check the level of the lower section, before fitting and mortaring in the top section.

quicker. Alternatively, you can tie in brickwork using brick galvanised "butterfly" ties.

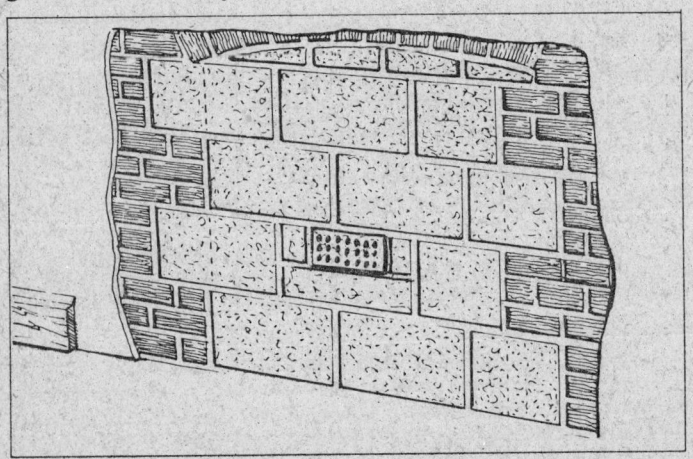

36. When a fireplace is bricked in, insert an airbrick in the lower portion to ensure a flow of air to prevent the build up of moisture and condensation.

Finally replaster the area. Insert an air brick in the lower half of the bricked-in fireplace to ensure air circulation, which will stop the formation of harmful condensation.

FIXINGS

Where walls are concerned, it might be remarked that custom cannot stale their infinite variety! This is certainly the case where choosing the correct method of fixing is concerned, so that what goes up – a wall cupboard or other fitments – stays up and does not come down!

The first rule is to check that it is a safe and secure point to fix anything. There must be no concealed cables or pipes; and the surface must be sound enough to hold the fixing device so that it will not pull out or work loose.

When drilling into hard wall surfaces, use a masonry bit. It will be easier to do the job with a power drill – but use this at a slow speed setting. Single-speed drills are usually too fast and will heat up and ruin the drill bit.

For really tough surfaces, use a power drill with a percussive attachment or setting. You must use a percussive masonry drill bit. Though the percussive action is simply a series of rapid but gentle vibrations as the drill revolves, this can dislodge the tip of an ordinary masonry drill.

Most wall surfaces will need drilling, then filling with a preformed plug. These are made of fibre, soft metal and synthetic resin and require a hole in the wall sized to the plug.

The screw gauge and depth should match the plug in ratio, or it may not grip. Plugs should be of the same length as, or slightly longer than the screw.

Fibre and soft-metal plugs grip the hole as they are expanded by the action of the turning screw. Nylon plugs have teeth or ridges which grip the sides of the hole as the screw is driven home.

You cannot use preformed plugs when fixing into hollow surfaces, such as plasterboard. A cavity type of fixing has to be used. There are various types, mostly made in nylon. These work broadly on the same principle – a toggle or expanding section which grips behind the hollow wall section, as shown in Fig. 37.

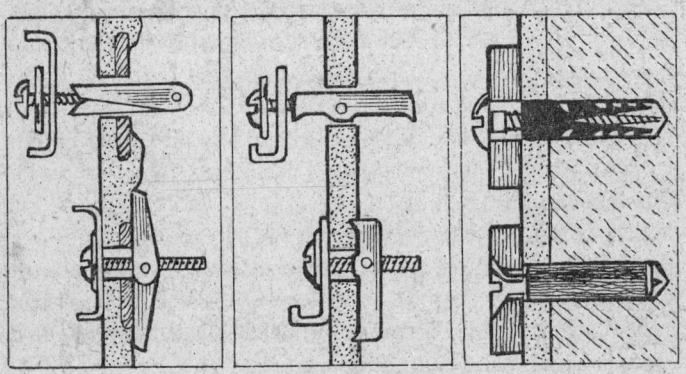

37. Four types of fixing device.
Left: A winged toggle for hollow walls.
Centre: A gravity toggle used in similar situations.
Right: A nylon and a fibre wall plug.

However, on hollow linings, try to screw-fix, at least in part, into the studded framework behind the surface.

Common screw sizes are Nos. 6, 8 and 12. Always gauge the screw-driver to the size of the screw head. There is a range of masonry drills to match screws.

Masonry or anchor bolts fix into hard wall surfaces and are used where heavier fixing is needed.

Aggregate has poorer load-holding qualities than brick or lightweight building blocks. Never fix in a friable surface. such as plaster. Drill through to a solid wall surface.

You can drill through ceramic tiles and similar hard surfaces, but stick a piece of tape to the surface and mark the drilling position with a cross. The tape stops the drill from slipping.

Some bits are supplied with a plastic depth gauge around the body. You can, however, make one up with masking tape.

Always ensure the drill bit is sharp. Squeaking, plus a drop in performance, shows bluntness, and this can overload a power drill.

Excessive speed will destroy the temper of the metal of the bit – it will turn blue and ruin the bit.

Blunted drill bits can be sent away to the manufacturer for re-sharpening.

Masonry nails

Masonry nails are of two types – one with a straight and the other a twisted shank, the latter giving better penetration into hard materials. There are three grades – standard, medium and heavy duty. Masonry nails should enter the surface squarely. Use a heavy hammer (an engineering type for preference).

These are used for fixing picture rails, skirtings, architraves, battens or "studs" for partitions. They are not suitable for holding shelving or cupboards. Use protective goggles when hammering home.

FLOORS – PREPARATION

Basically there are two types of sub-floor – solid, consisting of a concrete screed, and suspended flooring, timber or chipboard sheets nailed or screwed to joists. In very old premises, stone or quarry-tiled floors may be laid directly on to the sub-soil.

Solid sub-floors

These provide a good sub-surface for a range of flooring finishes, but must be clean, dry and level.

Small irregularities in the surface can be made good with a proprietary self-levelling compound, laid according to the manufacturer's instructions. This is not a durable surface and finish flooring should be laid as soon as possible after the compound has dried. The compound dries out quickly.

Repairs can be made using the same technique as that for making good concrete paths. For a perfect surface, make up the repair layer to just below the level of the surrounding screed, then lay a skim coat of self-levelling compound.

Hardboard can be used to provide a rigid sub-floor. On damp solid or suspended floors, use an oil-tempered grade. Ensure that the screed surface is clean, level and dust-free; allow new screeds up to three weeks to dry out.

Apply a proprietary adhesive to the floor with a notched spreader. Condition hardboard by standing sheets back to back at room temperature. On timber sub-floors, make sure that these are even and free of projections. Fix with 13mm hardboard nails at 150mm centres.

Hardboard may also be screwed down to provide easy access to underfloor services. Sheets may be stuck down with a flooring adhesive to a clean sub-surface. Where the hardboard is to provide a base surface for tiles or other flooring, it is easier to use small sheets of hardboard.

Suspended sub-floors

Timber is not inert and expands and contracts with fluctuating humidity. Small gaps between boards can be filled with wood filler or a papier-mâché mix, or small fillets of wood cut slightly oversize.

Stain papier-mâché to match the boards if they are to be prepared and left uncovered. Papier-mâché is made from newspaper soaked and mixed with glue size or cellulose based wall-paper adhesive. Smooth down filled areas.

Use tapered wood strips the thickness of the boards to fill larger gaps. Taper the strip with a plane and lightly tap into place; secure to the joists with 40mm panel pins.

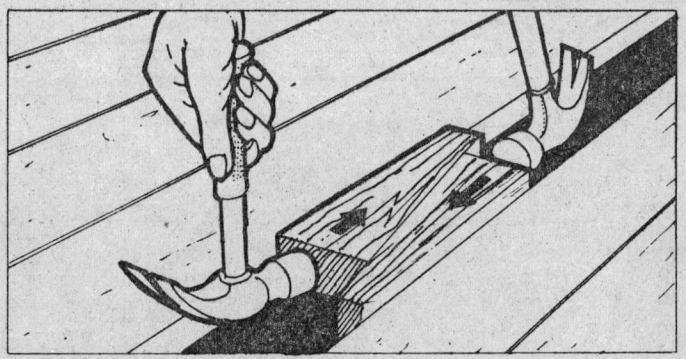

38. Use of wedges. When relaying boards, use two wedges as shown to cramp each tightly to the next.

Badly gapped boards can be covered with hardboard. Serious gaps or irregularities must be put right.

Before lifting floorboards, turn off the electric power in case electrical cables are run along beneath the joists. The position of the nails will indicate the direction of the joists, normally at 450mm centres and between 50mm and 75mm wide.

For recramping, which also provides an opportunity to replace worn floorboards, you need either a pair of flooring cramps (you can hire these), or you can use two tapered timber wedges to do much the same thing.

If flooring is tongued-and-grooved, cut through the groove on the first board with a slim chisel; this will enable it to be lifted. You may be able to prise up the board with a case opener and, using a scrap of timber as a fulcrum, bow the board from the middle, or you may have to cut the board, preferably across the middle of a joist.

39. A nogging. Noggings can be fixed to joists to secure a new section of floorboard.

If you have to cut elsewhere, you will need to insert a nogging, or cross-member, nailed between the joists afterwards to support the replaced board.

A floorboard saw, which has a curved blade, a power-saw or jig-saw or a keyhole saw can be used. You will have to drill a start hole for the keyhole saw but, if possible, cut at an angle, so that the replaced board fits snugly.

40. A floorboard saw. It has a specially curved blade.

When cramping to remove gaps, lift each board in turn, place it tightly against its neighbour and hammer in the tapered wedges with alternate blows from each end, or use floor cramps.

At the skirting, lever the last board tightly against its neighbour with a chisel. Fix boards with cut nails or with screws.

To fit a tongue or grooved board, cut off either the top or bottom lip of the tongued board to fit. You may have to adjust the size of the last board to accommodate this.

If floor boards are in good condition these can be smoothed and varnished to present a pleasing finish surface. Make sure that all nails are punched below the surface, holes filled and any old varnish, paint or grease is removed. A floor-sanding machine can be hired and used to produce a smooth finish.

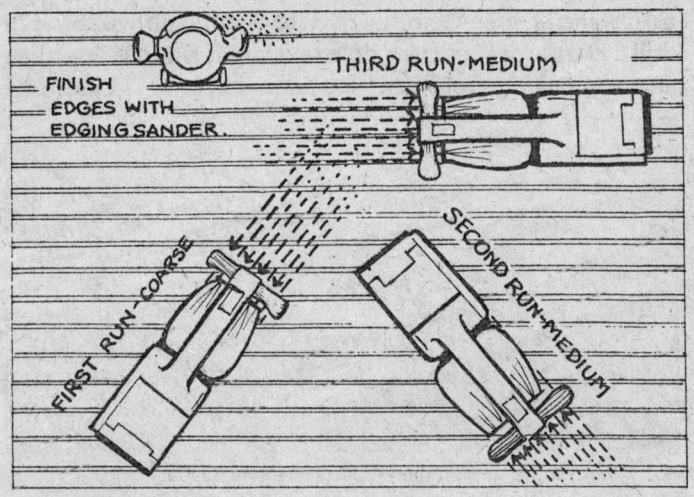

41. Smoothing a floor. The order of work and grades of glasspaper used at each stage.

Fit a coarse paper on to the drum of the machine. Start from one corner and work diagonally across the room. Pull the machine back after each "pass", then resand along the same line, overlapping by about 75mm. If the floor is very rough, repeat the sanding along the opposite diagonal, with a medium paper. Finally, fit a medium or fine paper to the drum and sand in one direction along the length of the boards.

Use a rotary sander, or finishing sander, with a fine paper at corners. Empty the sanding bag but do not burn the dust, for this will flare up.

If you have to replace a suspended floor surface, a flooring-grade chipboard, 20mm thick, will speed the work. Chipboard can be varnished as a finished surface.

Fix to joists with countersunk screws, staggering the position of the screws at the edges of the room to even stress. At the non-joist ends you may have to insert noggings, cross-pieces of timber between the joists, and screw the chipboard to these.

FLOORING MATERIALS

Before laying flooring, make sure that the sub-floor is in good condition. Concrete floors should be dry, clean and free from grease. Correct an uneven floor with a self-levelling screeding compound. Trowel this thinly over the surface.

Suspended floors tend to expand and contract and this can lead to gapping between boards. You can counteract this by laying a skin of hardboard. The sub-floor must be smooth and free from any sharp projections. You may have to repair damaged boards and knock down nails and screws.

Hardboard must be left for 48 hours in the room to adjust to conditions. Fix hardboard with 13mm hardboard nails at intervals of 150mm. Stagger the joints, and preferably use small sheets.

Ceramic and quarry tiles
These are best laid on solid floors but can be laid on firm timber surfaces. There are various grades of adhesive for the differing situations.

When laying tiles, you need a tile cutter, notched spreader, pincers (to nibble out shapes), a sponge or squeegee, for applying grout between the tile joints, and a soft cloth for polishing afterwards.

Lay tiles so that they line up evenly with the doorway and recede squarely to the far side of the room. Take a line from the centre of the doorway the length of the room, and mark this off in tile widths. Allow spacer gaps. At the position of the last full tile, mark another line at right angles to the first; this will provide a square corner from which to begin.

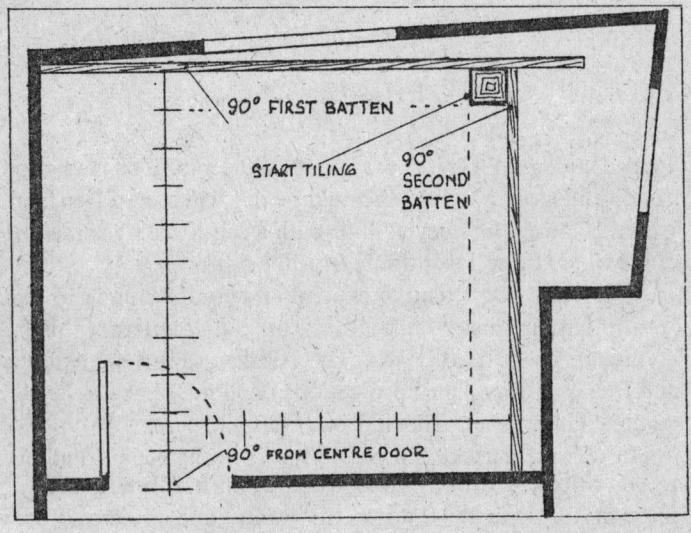

42. The method of setting out a tiled floor. Work to a right-angled batten to give a square starting point.

Apply tile adhesive thinly to the floor with the notched trowel and ensure that the main body of tiling is true. Tiles at the edges can be cut and filled in afterwards.

To cut an edge tile, place the tile face downwards over the gap and mark the waste line, then transfer to the front.

Score the tile, using a tile cutter and a straight edge. The tile will break when pressed down over a sliver of wood. You will need more pressure than when cutting a thinner wall tile.

Finally, grout the joints with a proprietary grouting, allow to dry and polish excess from the tile face.

Quarry tiles (carré, French, meaning square) are laid in a similar fashion. These are hard to cut and you may best do this using a power saw and a glass-fibre aluminium-oxide cutting wheel. Wear shatterproof goggles when cutting.

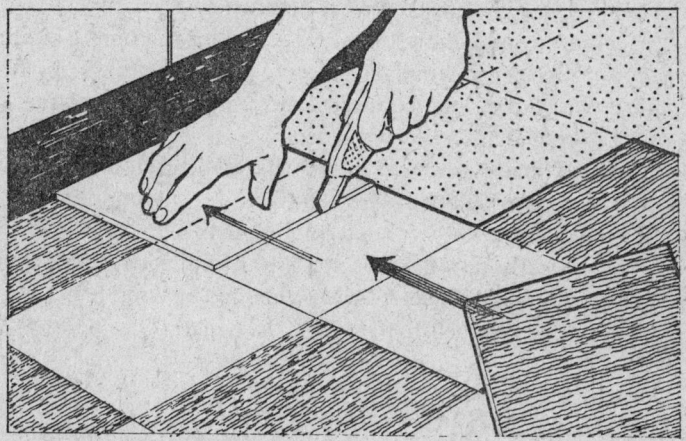

43. How to cut in for edge tiles. Temporarily place the last full tile in position, place another close to the wall and cut through the bottom tile. This tile should fit snugly to the wall.

Vinyl tiles

Find the room centre by "twanging" a chalked line to the floor — in the form of a cross. Lay a line of tiles "dry" from the centre. If this works out very unevenly, adjust the starting point. Tiles are laid from the centre outwards.

Lay a thin bed of adhesive for the first tile up to the chalked line. Position the first tile accurately on the chalked intersection and tile outwards to the walls. Butt tiles closely to each other.

At the wall edges, place the tile to be cut over the last full tile. Butt another tile against the skirting and over the second tile. Mark the overlap line on to the tile at the bottom. This will then profile accurately to the wall.

To cut vinyl tiles, you need a sharp handyman's knife with a lino-cutting blade. Score across the surface and snap cleanly. Lino tiles have to be cut completely through.

To mark round an architrave (e.g. a door surround), either use a proprietary template former, which contours to the shape, which can then be traced and accurately cut, or mark out the profile with a tile and a pencil.

Hold a spare tile upright, with one end touching the projection and the other over the tile to be cut, and mark off the projections point by point, join up, then cut.

Self-adhesive tiles must be stuck to a completely clean and dry surface. Merely peel off the protective backing paper and lay. Cut infill tiles before removing the paper.

Cork tiles
Lay these in a similar fashion to vinyl tiles. Use a recommended flooring adhesive. Roll after laying with a rubber roller to ensure that no air is entrapped. Cork tiles can be sealed or unsealed. Unsealed tiles have to be sealed with liquid vinyl or clear polyurethane – unless you wish to use a coloured polyurethane to obtain an interesting effect.

Sheet flooring
You require a pencil, a rule, a block of wood about 150mm long, a handyman's knife, with a lino-cutting blade, and a

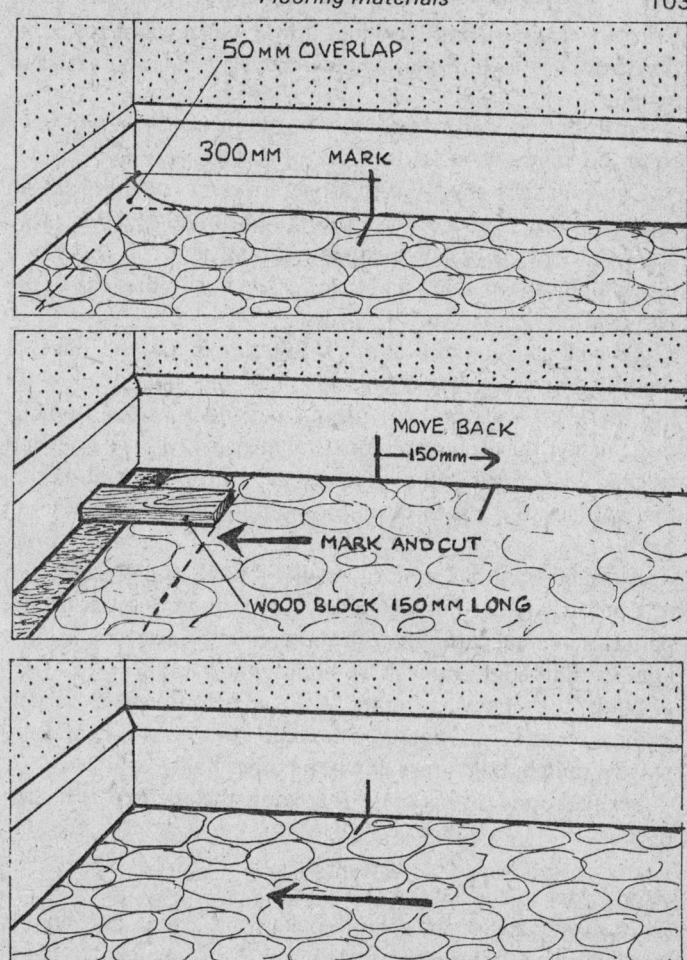

44. Laying vinyl flooring. Allow an overlap at wall ends on vinyl sheeting. Mark the wall and the vinyl as shown, pull back the length of the block and scribe a cut line. Finally, pull the flooring into place.

pair of scissors. Bring the vinyl into a warm room for some time before you start work. This makes it pliant and easier to handle.

As floor and wall angles may be out of true, you will have to scribe, in many cases, the flooring to fit.

Cut your first sheet 150mm oversize and lay this with an even overlap. If your flooring does not fit snugly at the wall along its length, pull it away by 75mm, and run the wood block along the skirting and transfer the line to the face of the vinyl with a pencil.

At wall ends, make a mark 300mm in on the base of the skirting and on to the vinyl. Pull the vinyl back until the mark on the vinyl is 150mm beyond that on the skirting, using the 150mm block to measure. Place one end of the block against the skirting, and, with a pencil, scribe the wall contour on to the flooring, cut, then slide the vinyl back.

If the flooring has a motif, you will have to pattern-match this before laying the next piece. Overlap and match up the pattern, then cut through both top and bottom sheets, using a long straight-edge and a sharp handyman's knife.

Stick the sheets together with a self-adhesive carpet-joining strip. Stick under one half of the join, carefully pattern match, then press down the other half.

Scribe round projections following the method used for tiles.

Woodblock

This may consist of solid blocks, end-grain, particularly hard-wearing, or veneer bonded to plywood blocks. Some of the latter are better for heavy wear than others. Woodblock flooring may be tongued and grooved, loose-laid or fixed down with a suitable adhesive.

Condition before laying by bringing into the room for up to a week.

Setting out

Divide the room in half. Mark a line in the centre of the doorway. Draw a line at right angles to this to the far side of the room. Work from the centre outwards. Allow a 13mm gap at wall edges. A cork expansion strip takes up movement. This is fixed down with adhesive.

In many instances, wood flooring will raise the level of the floor and you may need to remove skirtings. Lay the floor to the wall line allowing a 13mm expansion gap – which will be covered when the skirting is replaced.

Two effective designs are herringbone, which utilises a straight border at wall edges, and a simple chequer-board pattern – four strips of wood laid with alternating wood grain in each section. After gluing, punch two 25mm panel pins, one at each end, into each block to secure it, fill the holes with woodstopper.

Strip flooring

Start from the corner of the longest wall. Leave a 13mm expansion gap at the edge. Cut off tongues and grooves, at wall edges. Square the panels to the long wall and tap into place, using a hammer against a piece of scrap timber. Lay with the grain alternating.

Fit each cut-in piece, measured as for floor tiles, before the last panel to them is finally tapped into place. Fill in cut pieces progressively as you lay the main floor.

At the threshold, fix panels with adhesive or with 25mm pins, punched below the surface; fill the holes with a stopping or beeswax.

Use a diminishing strip where the levels between adjacent floors vary. This is a tapered piece of wood, grooved on one side, which is fixed to the sub-floor and butted up to the threshold panels.

On concrete floors, fix down with adhesive. On timber floors, fix with screws. If exposed, use brass screws and cups.

Allow the flooring to settle and then sand down with a rotary sanding machine. Either finish with wax polish or seal with a protective polyurethane varnish.

GARDEN SHEDS

A garden shed needs to be stood on a firm base with a damp-proof barrier beneath so that damp cannot rise and rot the timbers.

Either build a concrete raft or base or build up a pier of brickwork for the shed to stand on. Place bituminous felt beneath the shed timbers for damp protection.

Check the condition of shed roofing and replace with bituminous felt. You can apply a proprietary brush-on roofing liquid to repair damaged roofing felt, after brushing clean. These liquids are in a choice of basic colours.

Repaint or treat all wood surfaces regularly.

As added protection against damp and to protect the contents of your shed, line the inner surfaces with a bituminous paper.

GLASS

Glass is produced in a variety of thicknesses to suit a wide range of uses, such as the degree of exposure to which it is put and wind suction.

There are two types of glass – drawn sheet glass and float glass. Sheet glass is basically used for domestic glazing and is made in thicknesses from 3mm. It usually possesses some degree of distortion.

Sheet glass is produced in three grades: OQ (ordinary quality), SQ (selected quality) and SSQ (special selected quality). For most uses, the OQ grade is suitable.

Float glass has replaced plate glass and is produced by floating the liquid glass over a bed of molten tin. It is made in thicknesses of from 5mm to 25mm and is free from the distortion usual with drawn sheet glass.

You can also obtain tinted and coloured glass, patterned glass, wired glass, toughened glass, horticultural glass, the latter with good light-transmission qualities to promote growth, and diffused reflective glass, for glazing pictures.

Glazing is best done, if possible, in warm weather, when glass is less brittle.

When you order glass, give the height followed by the width. Particularly with ribbed and patterned glass, for the motif could be running the wrong way.

Take all measurements from the inside of each rebate using a steel tape. Frames can go out of square, so check the diagonal measurements as well. If you have an irregular shaped window to glaze, it is best to make up a template from cardboard.

When handling larger sheets of glass, wear gloves. These should not be too stiff, so that you can hold the glass firmly. As an alternative, make up "laps" of folded newspaper or use an old car inner tube.

Never grip glass tightly. Carry vertically — and never balance it on your head! You can, however, carry small sheets under your arm.

If you collect glass in a car, wrap it in a blanket and interleave each with newspaper. You can carry a large sheet on a roof rack. Lay it on blockboard and cover with a blanket. Lash firmly, drive carefully and avoid "crash" stops!

Store glass at an angle of 25°. Place on two wooden slats and separate with laps of newspaper.

Cutting

Though you can buy glass cut to size, it is not difficult to cut. It is advisable to protect the wrists and eyes when cutting glass. Tools required are glass cutter with a steel wheel and notches on the back (these are to check the gauge of the glass) and a draughtsman's tee-square — or a home-made one resembling this — is helpful to guide the cutter.

A pair of pliers is needed to trim off narrow strips of glass, and a steel tape or rule and a wax crayon are required for measuring and marking.

Lubricate the cutter wheel on a piece of felt soaked with oil.

Cut glass on a large flat surface covered with a blanket. Measure carefully and allow 3mm to the dimensions for the thickness of the cutting wheel. Lubricate the wheel and hold the cutter with the handle between the first and

second fingers. The bottom of the hand should be clear of
the glass.

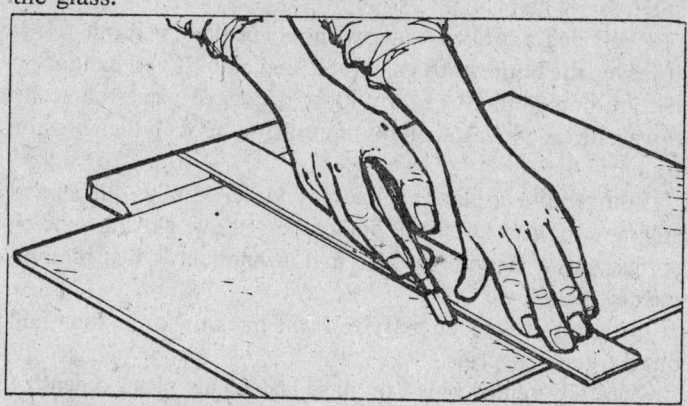

45. Cutting glass (i). Score along a straight edge. Do not back track.
Use a firm surface covered with a blanket. Tap the glass beneath
the score line to "open" it.

Score with a firm stroke, drawing back the arm, with the
body stiff, and do not back-track.

After scoring, lift the pane, tap gently from beneath along
the score line, place a batten or the cutter beneath the pane
under the line, then press down evenly on each side, to break
cleanly.

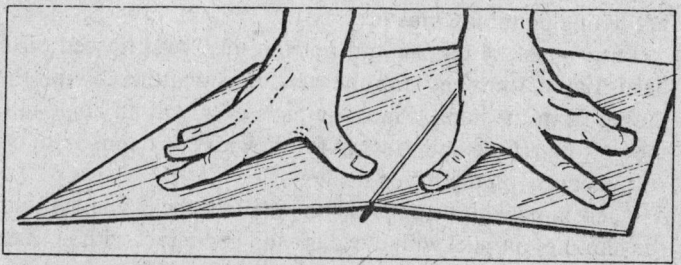

46. Cutting glass (ii). Press evenly on each side, with the glass cutter
beneath as a fulcrum to break.

To remove small strips, score as before and "nibble" off in small segments with pliers.

Replacing a broken window should be done without delay. It leaves the home both vulnerable and cold. If you cannot do the job immediately, remove loose or jagged pieces carefully — wear thick gloves — and temporarily tack polythene to the frame.

You require a glazier's hacking knife, to take out jagged splinters, or an old chisel, pincers to remove glazing pins or sprigs, and a cross-pein Warrington hammer, when pinning the new pane.

Loosen the exterior putty with the hacking knife, then pull out the glazing sprigs.

Carefully remove broken glass and finally clean down the rebate to bare wood. Smooth the rebate of the frame, using medium glasspaper and give it a coat of wood or metal primer, dependent on the window. Remove any rust with wire wool, then treat with a rust neutraliser.

When glazing windows of average size, cut the glass about 1.5mm under actual window size to allow for frame contraction. On large windows, double this allowance.

Glaze wooden frames with standard glazing putty. For metal frames and sealed double-glazed units, use non-hardening plumbing mastic.

Putty must be pliable and not too oily. Add linseed oil if hard. Lay a 3mm bed into the rebate, balling this in with the thumb from the hand. Place the pane evenly at an angle into the bottom rebate and press in firmly with one hand. Trim off surplus putty on the inside frame.

Tack in new glazing sprigs or pins into the frame, holding the hammer parallel with the glass and in contact with it. Start these with the cross-pein. Space them about 150mm apart.

On metal frames, clips and not sprigs are used. Save these

for re-use. Use plastic expansion pieces (available from glass merchants) along the bottom of the frame.

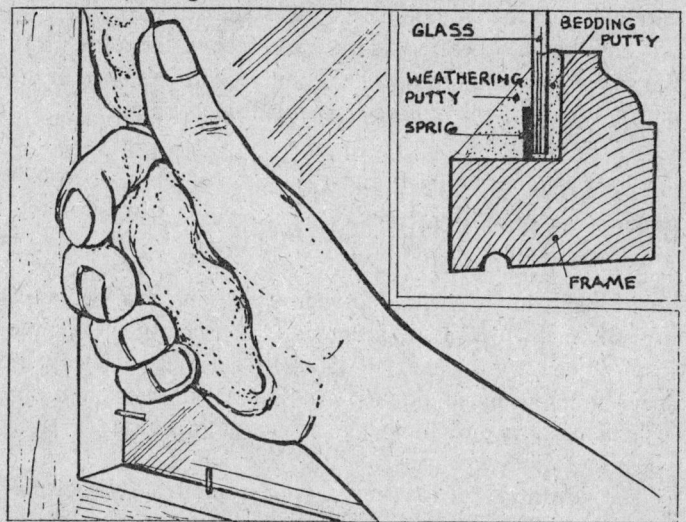

47. Applying the putty. Putty must be soft. Ball it in the hand and press the weathering putty in with the thumb. Smooth and mitre the four corners neatly with a putty knife. Keep this moist or it will lift the putty.

Finally, apply weathering putty to the outside. Smooth this to an angle of 45° using a putty knife. Keep the blade lubricated with water to stop the putty from sticking to the blade and pulling away. Trim each section with a single stroke and pare off surplus putty at the edges and mitre each corner. Go over the putty with a soft brush.

After about three weeks, apply a protective coat of paint on the putty and just on to the glass to form a seal.

If you need to cut a circular hole in a pane for an extractor fan, you require a radius-arm cutter, which has a central suction pad and is adjustable for size.

First, mark the outer circle, then an inner "safety" ring, 20mm inside this. Score the safety ring into segments. Tap carefully with the base of glass cutter to loosen the cut.

Cross-hatch score marks on the centre of the glass up to the safety ring and tap out the segments with the back of the cutter. Finally break out the segmented safety ring.

INSULATION (THERMAL)

Good insulation is a vital factor in preserving comfort levels in the home, while saving money and conserving energy. No form of heating is cheap. It is estimated that for every £1 spent in uninsulated homes 75p is wasted through roofs, walls and floors, up chimneys and via gaps around ill-fitting doors and window frames.

The advantage of looking at your home from the insulation view-point is that it can be a stage-by-stage process as funds allow.

Up to 20 per cent of heat loss is through the roof. Whether or not you have central heating, this large area should be insulated.

A loft can be insulated in two main ways – between the rafters, if the loft is to be used occasionally, or between the joists. In the former situation, it is not essential to insulate the cold-water cistern and pipes, for heat will still rise into the roof space, but if you insulate between the joists the roof becomes a cold area, both cistern and pipe runs must be lagged.

Leave out insulation beneath the cistern as this allows a limited amount of warm air to rise and helps to prevent the water from freezing.

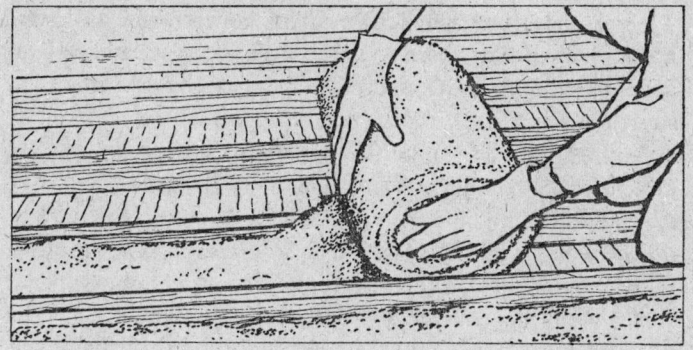

48. Rolling glass-fibre mat between joists. Use a minimum thickness of 75mm.

Among insulating materials are solid or loose-fill polystyrene, cork, mineral wool, glass-fibre and expanded ebonite. Fibre building board can also be used.

Blocks of polystyrene or mineral wool should be fixed between the rafters. Lay glass-fibre mat or mineral fibre quilt, of a minimum thickness of 75mm, between the joists.

49. Loose-fill insulation. A hardboard template is the best way to spread loose-fill insulation. Lay to a depth of 100mm.

Alternatively pour loose-fill insulant between the joists and cut a piece of hardboard to notch over the joists and provide a depth of 75mm—100mm. Plane this along the joists, as shown in Fig. 49.

Pipe lagging is usually in the form of a foam sleeve or a mineral wool bandage. You merely place the sleeving around the pipework and tape at intervals.

The walls in an older home usually are solid, while those in more modern buildings are of cavity construction. On solid walls, apply an insulant layer to the internal surfaces. You can use a polystyrene-backed cladding board. Usually this type of cladding is fixed on battens. Another method is to fix a layer of mineral-wool quilting behind battens then wood-clad these.

Polystyrene "wallpaper", sheet polystyrene 2mm thick, can be hung before you hang your lining paper. This will cut some heat loss and, more importantly, raise the "touch" temperature of the walls which helps to cut condensation.

Cavity walls can be filled with urea-formaldehyde foam or mineral wool. This is a specialist job as it involves drilling holes in the outer walls, inserting the insulant material under pressure and making good. If you build an extension, you can insulate the cavities with mineral-wool slabs and use thermally efficient lightweight building blocks for the inner skin. Both are aids to cutting heat loss.

Windows present an area of heat loss. Glass is a poor insulator and double glazing will certainly add to your comfort levels. This helps avoid draughty areas created when warm air reaches the cold window zone and eliminates condensation. However, double-glazing is expensive and needs to be budgeted for.

Gaps round the door can be eliminated with foam rubber or plastic self-adhesive strip. A more expensive method is to use sprung-metal strip which is pinned round the door frame at regular intervals and then sprung outwards, pressing against the closed door to make a firm seal.

This method can also be used for windows — but it is expensive. Some systems are fixed by specialist firms, others you can do yourself. Gaps round windows can be sealed with self-adhesive foam-rubber or plastic strips.

Suspended floors are often a source of draughts which blow up through gapped floor boards. If the gaps are large you may have to recramp the boards. Small gaps may be filled up with a papier-mâché type filler, made from newspaper, allowed to harden and sanded down, or fillets of wood cut to fit. A good underfelt and the best carpet you can afford will also help, or you might decide to have a wood or vinyl sheet-flooring finish.

Costs can be cut by insulating hot-water storage cylinders and hot-water pipe runs. Cylinders can be lagged with a "jacket" or "waistcoat". There are several proprietary makes available but these are basically segments filled with 25mm of mineral wool which fit with bands and clips round the cylinder. Some cylinders come already coated with a polystyrene jacket.

JOINERY — REPAIRS AND RENEWALS

Among the most common problems is the seasonal one of sticking doors and windows. Timber frames, after any lengthy damp spell, can absorb a great deal of moisture, causing the timber fibres to distend.

This can happen through the paint surface, for the fibrous

nature of timber admits some moisture, even with a protective film of paint.

The only solution is to allow the timber to dry out. If you plane the frame down, it will gap once the timber has dried out and the swollen fibres have subsided.

However, there may be a particular point of friction caused, perhaps, by a build up of paint. It is a simple matter to glasspaper the protrusion down.

Cracks between the constituent parts of a window or a door frame should be treated. Water can loosen glue and rot joints; in severe cases you may have to replace the entire frame.

Fill any frame gaps with an exterior grade of filler and repaint.

On broken joints you will have to take the frame apart, repair, and reassemble. Remove the glass carefully for re-use – see the section on glazing for replacing glass, page 107.

Mortice-and-tenon joints are commonly used on doors and windows. Some joints are fixed with wedges and others with dowels, or even a combination of both. You will have to strip back paint to locate dowel fixings, through the frame bottom rail face into the tongue.

Wedges are inserted above and below the end of the tongue of the joint to make a tight fit. Drill a small hole through the middle of each wedge and prise the segments out with a slim chisel.

Tap the frame apart carefully with a hammer, against a block of wood, so that you do not bruise the frame. Scrape off old glue; brushing with boiling water helps this. Clean up the joint with glasspaper.

A rotted or broken tenon will have to be replaced; use a fillet of hardwood for this. This should be of the same depth and thickness as the replaced tongue but twice its length.

Cut off the old tenon flush with the end of the rail, place the rail in a woodworking vice and measure the depth of the tenon back along the rail with a try-square and a pencil; mark across. Use a marking gauge to gauge a line on the rail the width of the tenon. Carefully cut out the slot and clean up with a chisel.

Drill dowel holes through the face of the rail, or use the existing ones. Drill corresponding holes through the new tenon, slightly displaced to the outside so that when the

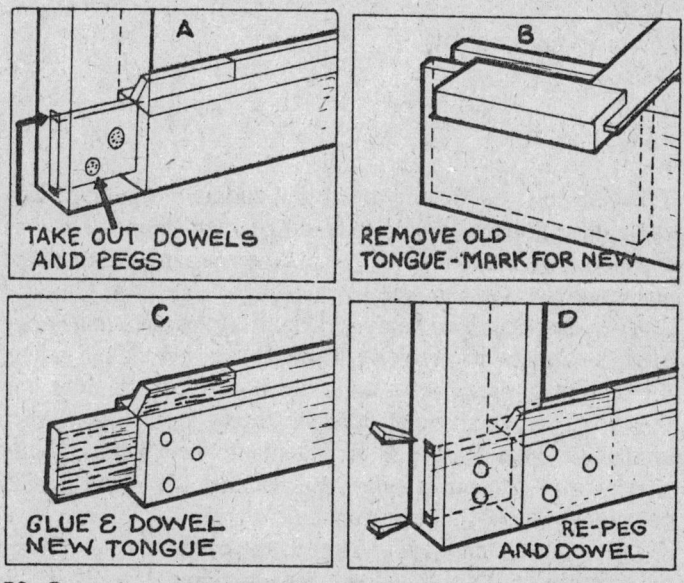

50. Renewing damaged joints. The four stages of removing and renewing a damaged joint on a window or a door frame.

dowels are tapped home, the tenon is pulled tightly into position.

Glue the tongue to the rail and glue and tap home new dowels. Make these slightly over-size; they can be trimmed after the glue has set. For this type of joint an animal glue is best. Cut small replacement hardwood wedges the thickness of the tenon, and glue and tap these in to make a firm joint.

When reassembling, you may need to use a pair of sash cramps to hold the frame true. Measure cross-diagonally both ways to check. These measurements should be the same.

For sash windows, see page 170.

KITCHENS

The kitchen is one of the most-used rooms in the home and as a central work area needs to be planned not only as ergonomically efficiently as possible, but as an easy to clean, attractive room in which to work.

Your first task is to analyse the existing space. An average kitchen can lend itself to one of three basic layouts – a galley, for the narrow area, with units down one or both sides, the U-shaped arrangement of units on three sides, in the larger kitchen, and the peninsular arrangement where a run of units also acts as a room divider or breakfast bar. This is also usually a basic U-shaped arrangement.

Draw out a plan of your kitchen to scale, on graph paper, cut out pieces of card to represent appliances, such as the cooker, washing machine and so on, and move them around until you produce the best possible arrangement. Try to eliminate unnecessary movement by keeping particular work areas together.

There are three specialised work areas: for food preparation, cooking and washing up. For the latter you will need a flat surface to stack dirty dishes, the sink and an area for drying.

It is a good rule to have a flat worktop between each appliance and these are essential next to the cooker or hobs and the sink.

Try to ensure that surface areas and storage are linked, so that your appropriate storage and related work areas are in job sequence.

As a lot of time can be spent working at and around the kitchen sink, where possible site the sink under or near a window, for light and the best view.

Kitchen storage usually consists of floor-standing cupboard units or open shelving. Units are generally between 760mm and 915mm high and 530mm deep. At least one drawer unit is useful for storing kitchen linen. High-level wall cupboards are usually best placed about 300mm above the work surface. Cupboards or open shelving may be used; though the latter are more easily accessible they may be less hygenic.

There is a wide range of ready-made kitchen units on the market, pre-finished or ready for you to finish. However, you may wish to cut costs and buy whitewood units which you can then paint, polyurethane varnish or laminate to choice. Both pre-finished and unfinished kitchen units can be bought in kit form.

For the completely non-standard kitchen, where buying units to a fixed module might waste space, you may prefer to make your own units in solid timber, whitewood, or veneered chipboard. Pre-made plastic drawer kits cut out one of the problems associated with precision carpentry and make even the beginner an expert. Work surfaces can be made of chipboard, laminated to choice, or you may prefer to use a finish such as ceramic tiles.

Avoid dangerous arrangements of equipment in the kitchen. Do not place a cooker underneath a window or next to a door opening. Keep electric points at least one metre from the sink. Try to avoid having doors facing one another. Not only does this waste space, but a through traffic-way can be potentially dangerous.

Wallcoverings in the kitchen should be easy to clean and, if possible, warm to the touch to reduce condensation. Wood panelling, washable wallcovering, or ceramic tiles are good wall surfaces. Flooring should be easy to clean and hard-wearing. Ceramic tiles, vinyl sheet or tiles, cork or linoleum are some of the materials you might use.

KITCHEN APPLIANCES

Two main kitchen appliances you may wish to install are a dishwasher and a washing machine. Many makes of washing machine enable you to make temporary connections to kitchen taps but it is far more satisfactory to plumb in permanently.

Some makes only need connecting to the cold supply, while others have to be plumbed in to both hot and cold services.

Cold water should come from the loft storage and this may require a separate supply. There is usually a supply of hot water to the kitchen sink and it is simple to tap this. Clip any new pipework firmly to wall surfaces at intervals.

To feed both a washing machine and a dishwasher, it is usually possible to connect to the same supply source. Give consideration to the location of these appliances, perhaps side by side beneath a continuous working surface and near the sink.

This will help in being able to make convenient connections to both supply and waste services.

Many makes of both washing machine and dishwasher connect to the supply with flexible hoses to the back of the appliance; the hose is pushed over the supply-pipe "tail" and a jubilee clip is tightened to ensure a water-tight joint.

The dishwasher will need similar connection to the hot and cold supply, but follow manufacturer's instructions as to fitting a water-seal trap and any other specific requirements.

You can extend pipework by fitting an equal tee-piece, to enable tails to be connected to kitchen tap, washing machine and dishwasher — observing the fact that you may not be allowed to connect the incoming mains other than to serve the kitchen tap, garden hose and replenish the storage cistern. Fit stop-cocks on the supply pipes so that you can shut these down if need be.

The flexible outlet hose usually has a crooked end which you loop into an air-break consisting of a vertical piece of 38mm waste pipe, clipped to the wall or a firm surface. The waste outlets can be taken to an outside trapped yard gulley. It is simple to make drainage connections with modern plastic plumbing.

Plastic connecting hoses are easily cut with a sharp knife — but leave sufficient so that the machines can be pulled out easily.

A 13A main supply is necessary for both appliances. Connections can be made to the ring mains in the usual way.

Waste-disposal units

Kitchen refuse disposal is an everyday problem and one of the most hygienic solutions is to install a waste eliminator.

Most waste can be ground into a slurry which is then washed down into the drain. However, it will not accept old cans, glass, or fibrous food waste, such as banana skins.

An eliminator has an electrically operated motor which drives an impeller and shredder blades. It requires a 13A power supply, and a pull-operated switch or a wall switch located well away from the sink.

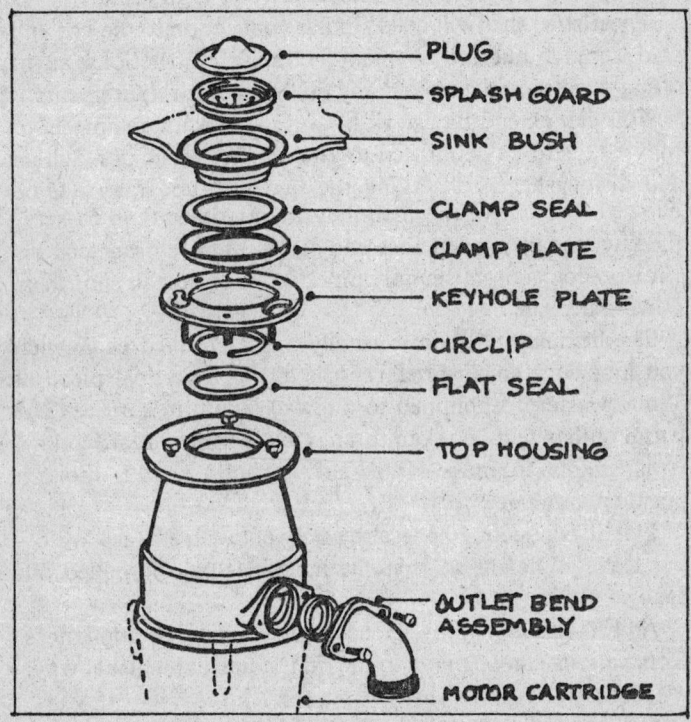

PLUG

SPLASH GUARD

SINK BUSH

CLAMP SEAL

CLAMP PLATE

KEYHOLE PLATE

CIRCLIP

FLAT SEAL

TOP HOUSING

OUTLET BEND ASSEMBLY

MOTOR CARTRIDGE

51. Waste-disposal unit. The assembling of a sink waste-disposal unit or eliminator. This connects to the sink waste outlet. (Econo-Parkamatic Ltd).

You can fit some models to a standard sink outlet. Others will require a new sink or the outlet enlarged. You cannot enlarge enamelled or vitreous sinks.

Fitting and adaptation of the plumbing-outlet arrangements are quite straight-forward, following manufacturer's detailed installation instructions. You must use a tubular trap and not a bottle trap for the latter encourages the formation of sediment.

The waste outlet should be taken into a trapped yard gulley, so that the slurry discharges under the water and does not leave any unhygienic surface deposit.

LAMINATES

In recent years, the widespread availability of laminates, in a wide variety of colours and designs, has done much to revolutionise decorative surfaces in the home. While the most obvious application has been to provide hard-wearing, easy-to-clean, wipe-down surfaces in the kitchen, laminates can be used most effectively in almost any room.

Laminates are produced in sheets 1.22m wide by 2.44m 2.74m or 3.05m. An extra-wide 4.12m × 1.52m sheet is also available. For use on surfaces that will take hard wear, use a 1.5mm-thick laminate. Plan carefully before you buy your materials as off-cuts can be bought at up to 50 per cent cheaper.

Laminate is usually fixed to a chipboard, plywood or blockboard surface, using either a contact adhesive, synthetic resin or epoxy resin. Apply the adhesive with a supplied spreader, thinly to the back of the laminate and the

52. Sticking laminates down (i). Apply contact adhesive to both surfaces, allowing them to become tacky. Position battens to keep surfaces apart, locate laminate accurately, then withdraw battens.

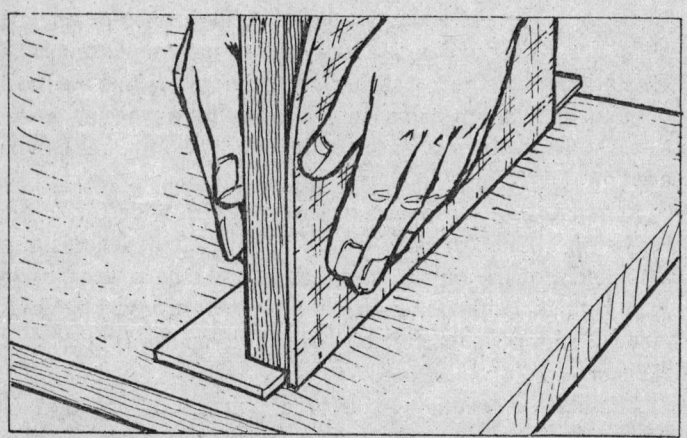

53. Sticking laminates down (ii). Another method is to locate the surfaces, after applying adhesive, over a batten, which provides an edging lip, then bring gently together.

base surface, and position the work carefully, for other than with a synthetic resin, adhesion is positive almost immediately the surfaces touch.

Allow contact adhesives to become touch-dry before bonding them together. Never fix to a dirty or greasy surface and if it has been painted or varnished, remove this before laminating.

Laminate can be either cut or sawn. You can use a laminate cutting knife to score deep lines into the surface, or a laminate cutter. A fine-toothed tenon or a power jig saw can be used for sawing. When sawing, make sure that the work is firmly clamped against movement, or you will split the laminate.

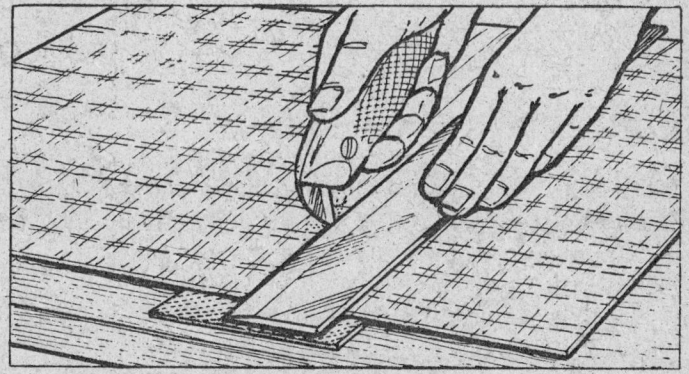

54. Cutting laminates. Score deeply or cut right through the laminate face. Use the correct laminate blade and do not back track in use. Place a protective scrap of material beneath the cut line. Bend laminate upwards to break evenly. .

If using a cutting knife, score the face side of the laminate. Score along the line of the cut, using a straight edge. Score until the dark inner core of the laminate shows. Either score right through or, with the straight edge in place, snap upwards to break the laminate cleanly along the line.

A thin, 1mm balancing, laminate should be used on the backs of surfaces, such as laminated doors, to counteract warp.

A laminate surface can be edged with matching laminate strips cut over size, stuck and then trimmed with a proprietary laminate edging trimmer, or can be bevelled with a block plane which gives a neat line, exposing the inner core.

Some of the many uses for laminates in the home, other than in the kitchen, are for bathroom cupboards, vanitory units, wardrobe surfaces, sink splashbacks and table tops.

LIGHTING

Planned lighting can provide three things – a good level of illumination, so that the light falls where it is needed, "mood" or atmosphere lighting, and safety, so that danger is highlighted.

Light is measured in lumens per sq. metre or lux, the amount of light falling on to a surface.

Varying levels of lighting are required in different areas of the home, from good, direct lighting for sewing or reading, to "mood" lighting quite adequate for entertaining and relaxing.

If you rewire your home also make a lighting plan to include details of the light fittings and position of lamps in each area. Forethought helps to avoid trailing wires, which are both unsightly and dangerous, and power points sprouting clusters of adaptors.

There are five main types of light fitting which can be categorised by design and the type of light distribution — direct, semi-direct, diffusing, semi-indirect and indirect.

A spotlight or angled lamp will give a good direct light for reading. The light throw is reflected down by the shade, localised and may produce glare unless used in conjunction with low-level background lighting. A pearlised bulb may also reduce glare.

Semi-indirect light fittings direct between 60 and 90 per cent of the light downwards, though light is also radiated in all directions. A softer light is produced by using toned or translucent shades.

Diffused light is a soft light which spreads in all directions, giving good, general illumination.

Semi-indirect fittings direct between 60 and 90 per cent of the light upwards, dependent on the shade chosen and are the most common type of light fitting. Semi-indirect wall light fittings or lamps may also be used for "mood" lighting.

Completely indirect lighting fittings also throw up to 90 per cent of the light upwards and a rather flat, shadowless light is produced.

Indirect light, from a concealed source, may be used to highlight a feature of architectural interest or a particular décor effect in any area.

In work areas such as the kitchen, a shadowless light may be desirable. Small strip lights can be fixed under high-level units to give localised work-surface light.

Spotlights over the sink and main work area provide localised lighting. These may be wall-mounted or fitted to ceiling tracks.

Fluorescent tube lighting gives a good shadowless light. If the ceiling is high it can be lowered by installing an illuminated ceiling of translucent PVC panels, inserted into a latticework of light-weight aluminium framing. These are top-lit by fluorescent light.

While colour effects can be produced by lighting, basically this can only be achieved by using coloured shades or coloured filament or tinted fluorescent lamps. Choose the colours carefully for they will in turn have different effects on furnishings and décor.

Tinted strip lighting can be used to create a warm tone in a living area or to highlight shelves, curtains and alcoves.

Illumination also depends on the reflective surfaces in the room. Light is reflected from the walls and ceiling. Lighter matt surfaces reflect most light. If the surfaces are dark, you will have to increase the light output.

Dimmer switches can be used to control the light level on main lights or lamps, which can mean a saving in electricity consumption.

Lighting can make an important contribution to home safety. Stairs should be well illuminated, lit from the top so that the stairway nosing is highlighted. Additional light may be necessary from a lower level so you get a balanced effect. During the night provide low-level lighting on landings and in hallways, particularly if there are children or older people in the house. If stairways have no natural light, it may be necessary to keep these lit all day.

Recessed lighting may save space, particularly where there is low headroom. This type of fitting can give direct or indirect light.

Plan for flexibility in lighting. In a main living area you will probably want fixed units, adjustable spotlights and portable lamps. Adjustable, pendant direct-light fittings, are good for use over a dining area. To cut glare, control with a dimmer switch or also provide other low-level background lighting.

Unless the bathroom is large, one central ceiling light will normally be sufficient, with localised light provided over a vanitory unit or shaver mirror. All lights must be pull-switch operated.

An illuminated ceiling works well in a bathroom.

Check outside lights. These should have weatherproof fittings and be earthed. Exterior lights can be a safety aid illuminating steps and pathways.

LOFTS

In many homes the loft is wasted space that could be used for storage or as an extra activity area. Other than for storage, you will have to lay floorboards or sheet flooring and in some instances strengthen the joists. Any structural alteration will require local authority planning consent and must conform with the Building Regulations.

Under the latter a habitable room, which is any room other than a kitchen or scullery, used for dwelling purposes, must be at least 2.3m high. Beams may be lower than this but no lower than 2m. Roof rooms may have sloping roofs or partially lowered ceilings provided the height, over at least half of the room, exceeds 2.3m.

In general, the main opening window or windows of habitable rooms must have 3.6m of open space, outside the window, and within the boundary of the home. Ventilation is required through one or more opening windows, or other ventilation openings, totalling in area at least 1/20th of the floor area of the room. Some part of this must be at least 1.75m above the floor level.

It is also possible to provide mechanical ventilation by an air conditioning unit or a ducted extractor fan system which is linked to the lighting.

LOFT LADDERS

A retractable loft ladder will give safe access to the roof space. Check that the loft opening is sound and will take the weight of the ladder and a person on it.

Also check that there is sufficient room for it to retract when not in use.

You may have to enlarge a small loft opening — a typical ladder requires an opening of at least 685mm × 500mm. Take care not to weaken the structure, if you cut joists. Lap new sections in. Make the hatch cover as light as possible.

Fixing details are supplied for the particular unit you buy.

METRICATION

A large proportion of the products used in building and home repairs and improvements are now sold in metric form. Many of the metric units correspond closely with the former imperial values.

It is easier and simpler to work in metric. It will be handy to have a steel rule, providing both metric and imperial dimensions, so that you can convert if necessary.

Linear

The basic linear metric units are the *millimetre* (written mm), *centimetre* (cm), equivalent to ten millimetres, and the *metre* (1000mm). Do not put commas between the multiple numbers.

A *metre* can be expressed as 1m, 1 metre, 1000mm or 100cm. Intervening numbers can be written as 1.5 metres or 1500mm or 1.500m, 1.5m, 1500mm or 150cm.

As a rough guide, 300mm is roughly 12in, a metre is just over a yard — 39.2in — and a *kilometre* (100 metres) is five-eighths of a mile.

Volume

There are three units, the *millilitre* (ml), the centilitre and the *litre*. The smallest usual size of container — for a product such as paint — is 100ml, equivalent to 0.18 pints. A *litre* is 1.76 pints, and there are roughly 5 litres to a gallon (1.1 gallon). One thousand millilitres equals one litre.

Area
This is expressed by the *Square metre* (m^2). (The cubic metre, (for volume), is written thus – m^3). The unit for large areas is the *hectare* (ha). One hectare is equal to about $2\frac{1}{2}$ acres.

Weight
Expressed by the *gram*, for small measures, and *kilogram* for larger quantities; 2 lb. represents roughly a kilogram. The *metric tonne* is equal to 1000kg, just under the imperial ton.

Timber
This is sold in 300mm lengths, starting at 1800mm. Sizes are roughly equivalent to imperial sizes: 12mm is roughly $\frac{1}{2}$ in., 25mm (1 in.) 50mm, (2 in.), 75mm, (3 in.), 100mm (4 in.).

Wallboards, hardboards and sheet plastics
The general sizes for these are:

1800mm × 900mm	2400mm × 1200mm
1800mm × 1200mm	3000mm × 1200mm

Plastic rainwater goods
Sold in 2m and 4m lengths.

Plumbing
Plumbing pipe is usually sold in 3m lengths. Standard sizes are 15mm ($\frac{1}{2}$ in.), 22mm ($\frac{3}{4}$ in.) and 28mm (1 in.) and 50mm (2 in.). Sizes 15mm and 28mm are compatible with the imperial sizes – where you have to join to existing pipework.

Heating units

The BTU/h (British thermal units per hour) is being replaced by the *kW/h*. The kW is 1000 watts. One watt is equivalent to 3.512 BTU/h.

Electrical cables

With the bonus of an international colour standard, fixed cables now have the strand thickness expressed in cross-sectional area in metric. Formerly, these were given in the number of strands with their thickness in fractions of an inch. Lighting cable was, for example, expressed 3.029, meaning 3 strands, each .029 in. in diameter.

There is now only a single strand of metric cable. Basic sizes are $1mm^2$ (lighting), $1.5mm^2$ (light power), $2.5mm^2$ (ring mains) and $4mm^2$ upwards for cookers.

Ceramic tiles

The basic sizes are 108mm × 108mm and 152mm × 152mm, unchanged from the imperial $4\frac{1}{4}$ in. × $4\frac{1}{4}$ in. and 6 in. × 6 in. tiles.

Glass is no longer measured in weight per sq. ft. but, more logically, by thickness. It is priced in m^2.

Metric	2mm	3mm	4mm	6mm
Weight	18 oz.	24 oz.	32 oz.	plate or float

Sand and ballast are sold by the metric tonne but small quantities may still be sold in gallons, bushels and cubic yards (yd^3).

Ready-mixed concrete is sold by the cubic metre.

Cement and plasters are supplied in 50kg bags (about 110 lb.).

Tools are mostly dual marked to indicate metric and

imperial equivalents. Drill shank sizes are shown in metric.

Door and window joinery, bricks, roof tiles, sink tops, kitchen units and sanitary ware are among many other products available in metric modules.

PAINTING

A painted surface is only as good as the preparation, and a poorly prepared surface will soon deteriorate. Preparation, though perhaps, tedious, pays off in a good long-lasting surface.

Avoid working in wet conditions, and never paint out of doors when damp or very hot, or your paint surface will suffer.

Preparing larger areas
Never paint on a dirty, dusty, greasy or unstable surface. Imperfections, such as paint curtaining, blistering and crazing, should be removed and made good before you repaint.

Before painting a wall, cut back and fill any plaster cracks. Wash down dirty surfaces with a detergent solution, starting at the bottom to avoid streaking, then rinse off finally with clean water.

Surfaces
Good paintwork will only need lightly rubbing down with fine glasspaper, dusting clean, then repainting. If the surface is chipped or blemished, fill with cellulose filler and rub down smooth with the surface, remove dust, then repaint.

Clean any rust from metal windows and doors with wire wool. Heavy rusting may cause frames to warp and have to be replaced. Apply a rust solvent, making sure that you have treated all rust before repainting.

On new or stripped wood, you will have to apply shellac knotting to any knots or resinous patches, prime, undercoat and then top-coat.

Polyurethane-based paints do not require a primer on wood but can be applied coat on coat, with the initial coat diluted by 50 per cent with white spirit.

A primer seals the base surface. Use the correct primer – oil-based wood primer on timber or aluminium primer on resinous wood and metal primer on metal. On weathered zinc, steel, aluminium or galvanised steel, use a zinc-chromate primer. On new zinc or galvanised metal, use a calcium-plumbate primer.

Avoid lead-based primers as these are toxic and dangerous to children.

Removing paint

Paint can be removed by one of three methods: by heat, chemically or by mechanical means. The easiest way to heat paint is with a butane gas blow torch, fitted with a flame-spreader head, and a paint scraper. However, avoid using heat near windows as this may crack the glass.

Paint scrapers are of various types. One type has a double-sided blade, with a serration on one edge to cut through paint film. Use a shave hook for paint-stripping in awkward places, such as mouldings.

Play the flame from side to side, taking care not to char the wood. Hold the stripping knife at an angle so that hot paint does not fall on to your hand. Start at the bottom of the area, and strip a small amount at a time. Afterwards, rub down with fine glasspaper.

Chemical strippers are produced in jelly or liquid form. A

jelly-type stripper is easier to use. Wear gloves and apply the stripper with an old paint brush. On stubborn surfaces, you may have to apply more than one coat.

These strippers give off a flamable vapour, so always ensure adequate ventilation. Do not use near a naked flame. After using a chemical stripper, wipe down the surface with white spirit.

55. Removing old paint. Use a flame spreader head with a butane torch and paint scraper to remove paint. Keep the flame moving just ahead of the scraper. Near glass, use a chemical paint stripper.

How to paint
For painting you need the following — paint, brushes or a roller and tray, a paint kettle, a clean cloth and a "tack"

cloth, white spirit and sound access equipment. The "tack" cloth is slightly tacky and effectively removes dust from the surface.

Before painting, make sure the area is as clear as possible and well ventilated. Aim to keep the equipment you are using and the surfaces to be painted as dust-free as possible.

All paint, other than gell or thixotropic, must be stirred thoroughly before use. If there is a skin on the top of the paint remove this. Do not attempt to mix it in with the paint. Mix either with a piece of clean wood, or with a paint-stirrer attachment fitted to a power drill. The right consistency is reached when the paint flows evenly from the tip of the stirrer.

Distil the amount of paint you need into a paint kettle. This avoids carrying a heavy tin of paint, with the risk of spillage and wastage. Polyurethane paints have a limited "wet-edge" time and if you experience paint drag on the brush, add a little white spirit.

A four-coat system of painting is best on bare softwood. Apply primer and either two undercoats and one top coat, or one undercoat and two top coats. Allow the primer to dry for at least 48 hours, lightly rub down with a medium-grade wet-abrasive production paper, then wipe down with a damp cloth. Rubbing down between coats aids adhesion.

The undercoat – which should be in the same colour range as a top coat – has more colour pigment than the final coat and provides a dense base. Do not apply the paint too thickly as this may "curtain" or "sag". Spread the paint as thinly as possible, while maintaining an even colour density.

Keep the surface free of brush marks, for an uneven undercoat will show through the top coat. It may be best to apply two undercoats and one top coat. Undercoat takes between 16 and 20 hours to dry. Rub down lightly between coats with fine glasspaper, clean off with a tack cloth, then apply the top coats. Gloss paint takes up to 24 hours to dry completely.

Gell paints have a good covering capacity; one coat is equal to a thin undercoat *and* a top coat of conventional paint. Apply and lay off in the same way as for gloss. You will find the brush needs to be charged more frequently.

When applying two top coats, it is best to use one eggshell and one gloss finish. For interior work, use eggshell, semi-gloss or full-gloss finishes. Full gloss is harder wearing and is best used where the surface is exposed to strong sunlight or condensation.

The right brush

The best brushes possess real bristle filling. Bristle has tiny barbs which hold the paint. Cheaper nylon fillings, which are smooth, have poorer paint-holding qualities. However, a nylon brush is useful when applying water-based paints as it is easier to clean.

Flex a new brush against the palm of your hand to remove dust and loose bristles. Use a new brush initially for under-coating and not for top-coating.

Charge the brush by dipping the filling into the paint for about two-thirds of the bristle length, then touch against the side of the kettle to remove excess paint. Subsequently, you only need dip the brush to a third of the depth.

Try to work in good natural light. Hold the brush in a relaxed manner, and control the movement by your hand and wrist. Brush up and down, then diagonally and finally across the grain. This four-way sequence gives an even paint spread. Lay off across the grain, one brush width at a time, to produce a smooth finish.

Work in a continuous sequence, for if you stop demarca-tion lines will show.

Never try to hurry the job by applying one thick coat — two thinner coats will give a better-wearing and smoother finish.

When decorating a room, start with the picture rails and skirting boards, then paint windows and doors.

Windows and doors

Before painting doors and windows remove all fittings, for paint is difficult to clean off afterwards. Paint in the order shown in Fig. 56 to 58.

Flush doors are difficult to paint as one area. Divide horizontally into three sections. Use a 75mm wide brush and start work in the top left-hand corner. Paint a wide

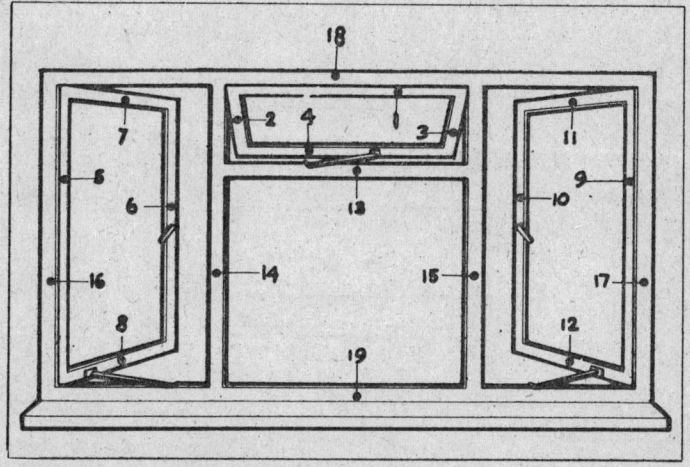

56. Painting order for a casement window.

vertical strip, then another parallel with the first. Brush across the two strips evenly into each other and "lay off" vertically, then repeat for the other sections.

Finally, brush lightly upward and downward, to join the sections. You will need to work quickly, particularly if using a quick-drying paint.

For painting large areas, such as ceilings and walls, use a roller or a large brush.

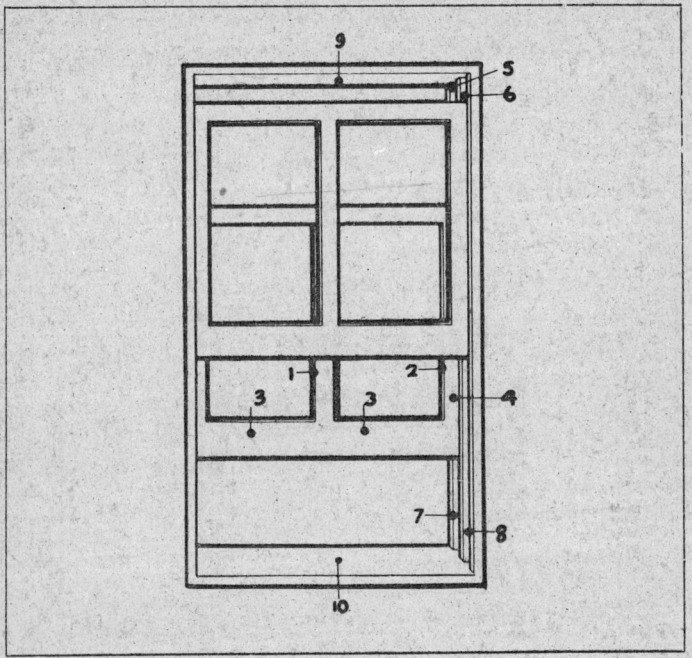

57. Painting order for a double-hung sash window.

Paint faults

Faults, such as blistering, crazing and bubbling, if not too severe, may be rectified without having to strip the entire surface. Rub down the blemish and feather the edges with glasspaper then fill with a cellulose filler. Rub down level with the surrounding surface, and repaint. If the paint surface is crazed, generally occurring when two coats of entirely differently constituted paints have been applied, the surface must be stripped back completely.

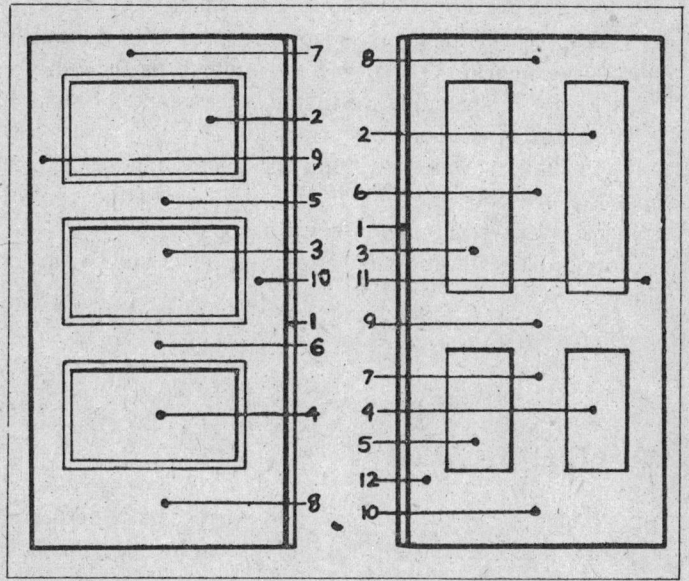

58. Painting order for a panelled and a cruciform door.

Dents in external timber can be filled with hard stopping or oil-based putty, stained to match the wood. First prime, fill, then rub down level with the surrounding area, prime again, and finally paint.

Brush care

Good brushes are expensive and it pays to take care of them. After use, make sure that they are cleaned thoroughly. Use white spirit to clean off other than water-based paints which can be cleaned by washing under the tap. Do not allow the paint to dry or you may not be able to remove it.

Before storing a brush make sure the filling (e.g. bristle) is dry. Wrap the brush in newspaper, secured with an elastic band, store in a dry place and put moth balls in with the brushes — for moths enjoy the filling! Never stand a brush on its filling, as this will bend or "cripple" it.

If you have stopped painting for a few minutes, either clean the brush or suspend it in a solution of the correct cleaner for the type of paint you are using.

Clean rollers thoroughly after use, dry, and wrap in newspaper.

PAPER-HANGING

Paper-hanging can be divided into three separate stages: preparation of the wall surface, lining, and hanging the final decorative covering.

Always work with as much of the room cleared as possible and use the right access equipment.

Do not paper over newly-plastered walls. For the first six months, use a water-based paint, such as an emulsion, to allow the plaster to dry out.

Never paper over distempered walls; distemper must be removed. You can paper over oil-based paint, but rub down first with a wet-abrasive paper.

You will need the following tools for wall preparation and paperhanging: sponge, plumb-bob or long spirit level, paper-hanging shears, or wheel cutter, straight edge, pencil, seam roller, smoothing brush, paste brush, scraper, paste table, a plastic bucket, access equipment — either two trestles and a scaffold board or, for a stair-well area, a lightweight tower or combined ladder and trestle system.

Sizing surfaces

Before hanging a lining paper, size the walls to seal the surface, and give a smooth surface on which to slide the paper. Use thinned glue size if using water-based adhesive, add a handful of whiting if applying to an oil-based paint area, and a thinned coat of cellulose adhesive if using cellulose adhesive.

Remove old wallcoverings, for it is not a good idea to paper on paper. Score the surface of the paper and soak with hot-water detergent solution, or you can use a proprietary stripper. For large areas, it may save time to hire a steam stripper. Tough papers may need several soakings.

Work from the bottom of the walls, and strip with a scraper, held at a shallow angle to the wall. Do not dig into the paper or you will damage the plaster. Rub down the area carefully with a medium glasspaper. Vinyl papers are easily stripped. Peel away one corner of the vinyl coating and pull it away, leaving the backing paper as a lining paper.

Double-line badly blemished walls, horizontally, with heavy brown or white glazed lining paper, and then line vertically.

Paper is generally in rolls 10m long and 530mm wide. A standard roll should cover an area of about 5.2 metres square used on a flat surface, allowing for pattern matching and trimming.

Estimating for wallcovering

Measure the height of the room and work out the number of lengths you can cut from each roll. Allow for pattern matching. Multiply the number of lengths by the trimmed width of the paper and divide this figure into the perimeter of the room.

Unless you have extra large windows, ignore these and doors when calculating your requirements.

It pays to buy the best paper you can afford; cheap papers may fade and tear easily. Allow extra for pattern matching.

Patterns may repeat horizontally or on the drop. The manufacturer will give these details, and for semi-plain patterns, some of which are hung with alternate lengths reversed. Most machine-printed papers are ready trimmed.

Buy enough paper to complete the job, for colours may vary slightly from batch to batch. Shading difficulties on plain or random-patterned paper can be overcome by hanging in alternate lengths.

Before papering, you must mark out an accurate vertical datum line, for walls are seldom true. Use a plumb-bob or a spirit level and pencil or a chalk marker to do this. Mark a vertical line at each corner of the room as a reference point when hanging.

Mark a vertical line about one metre away from a main window and begin from here.

For a paper with a large motif where there is a large chimney breast, paper this first, so that it looks symmetrical.

Cutting paper

Measure the length of the drop and unroll the paper on to the pasting table. Allow 50mm at each end for trimming. You can use paperhanging shears to cut the paper, or tear it against a metal straight-edge. On patterned papers, find the main motif, and cut the paper 50mm above this, adding 50mm to the length of the drop.

Adhesives

Use the correct adhesive for the paper. Most papers are hung with starch flour or cellulose paste. Use fungicidal pastes in areas of high condensation and for hanging vinyls.

Work in a good light. Paper-pasting techniques are the same for both lining and decorative papers.

Place the paper face downwards on the table, with the far end of the paper lined up with the end of the paste table and let the rest of the length drop on the floor. Allow a slight overlap on the far side to prevent adhesive seeping on to the face of the paper.

Put the adhesive near the table and stretch a piece of string taut between the bucket-handle sockets. Use this as a brush-rest and to wipe off surplus adhesive.

59. Pasting. Use a pasting table, positioned in good light. Paste each half of the drop in turn, from centre outwards to the edges.

Paste half the length at a time. Work from the centre of the paper outwards to the far edge. Spread thinly and evenly; move the paper towards you and paste towards this edge so that half the paper is pasted.

Fold the pasted section, paste to paste, to the centre and do not crease the fold. Move the paper along the table so that the folded loop hangs over the far end of the table and paste and fold the other half of the length in the same way.

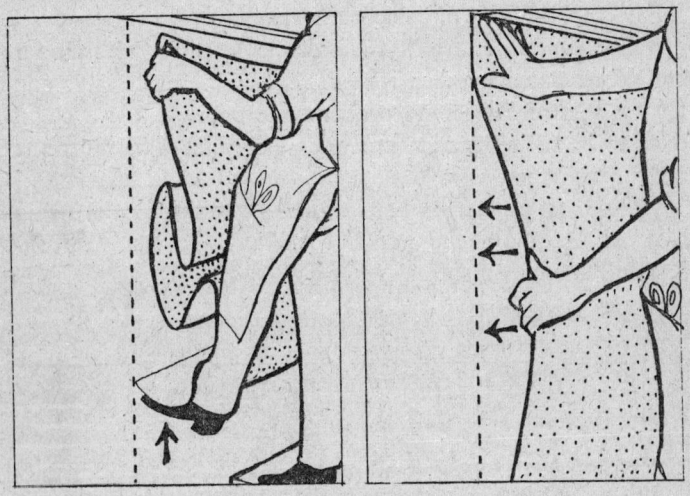

60. Hanging the paper. Overlap and carry over the arm to the wall. Position, then open out, supporting the lower part with knee and foot. Slide the paper into the vertical line or butt to previous drop.

Vinyl papers can be hung immediately but with other papers allow the adhesive to soak in for a few minutes. Concertina folding, used on long lengths for walls or ceiling lining is pasted in the same way, but with the paper looped in 300mm folds.

You need a small pair of steps when hanging paper. Carry the looped paper over your arm, unloop one half of the paper and position the top, allowing the 50mm trimming overlap to the top of the wall or picture rail and slide the paper up to the vertical line.

Support the lower fold of paper on your knee. Brush out the paper, from the centre outwards. Open out the bottom loop and brush out.

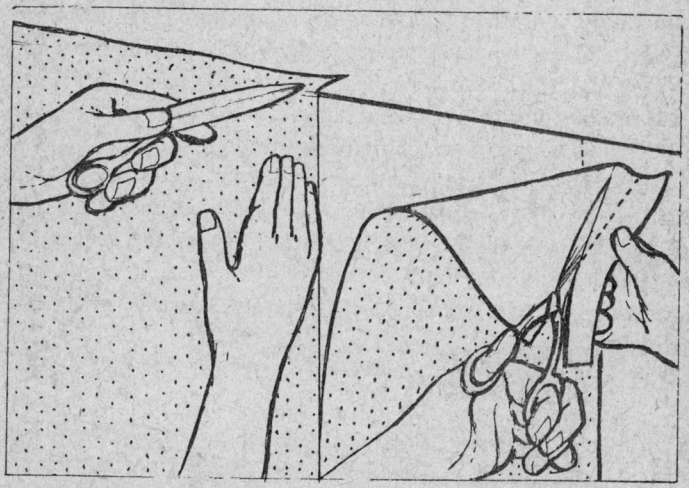

61. Ceilings and floors. Score the overlap at top and bottom with the back of the shears, then trim to the contour. Alternatively, use a cutting wheel to trim off excess.

Push the paper into the angle between the wall and ceiling or picture rail with the back of the shears. Pull gently away from the wall and trim along this line.

Alternatively, trim with a cutting wheel, run along the angle between wall and ceiling. Then smooth back. Similarly trim the bottom edge. Butt joins so the edges of adjacent pieces of paper meet exactly.

After about 10 minutes, roll the seams with a boxwood roller. On a flock or embossed paper use a rubber roller, a roller covered with chamois or a soft cloth.

Doors

Hang the last full width with a 25mm overlap at the top and door edge. At the top of the door frame, make a 6mm diagonal cut in the paper. Use the smoothing brush to push the paper into the angle between the door frame and the wall, crease with the back of the shears, trim and press back. Trim top and bottom. If the door opening is wide you may have to cut a short length of matching paper to fill in.

Paper a bay window or a recess, at the same time as the wall above it. You must cut separate pieces of paper for the reveals. Whether you work inwards towards the reveal or outwards from the inner corner of the reveal depends on whether you are working progressively towards or away from the reveal.

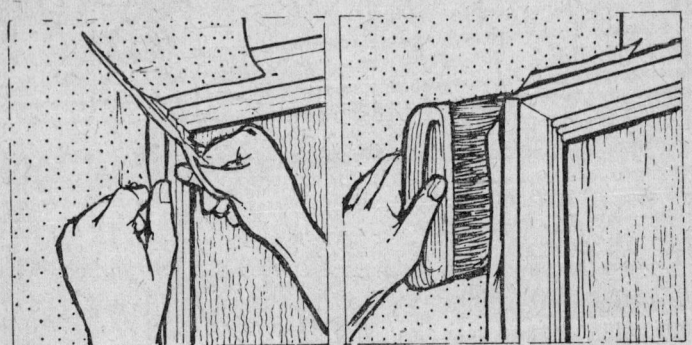

62. Doors and windows. Cutting and trimming in paper around a door or window frame.

Working outwards

Measure from the inside edge of the reveal round the corner. Allow for trimming if the outer edge of the reveal is not true. Align the outer edge of the paper vertically and mark this line. Paste the length and cut to the depth of the reveal, allowing 6mm above.

Smooth the paper into the reveal and trim at the vertical inner edge as necessary. A slight overlap will be left at the top of the reveal. Finally, trim round window boards and at the skirting edge.

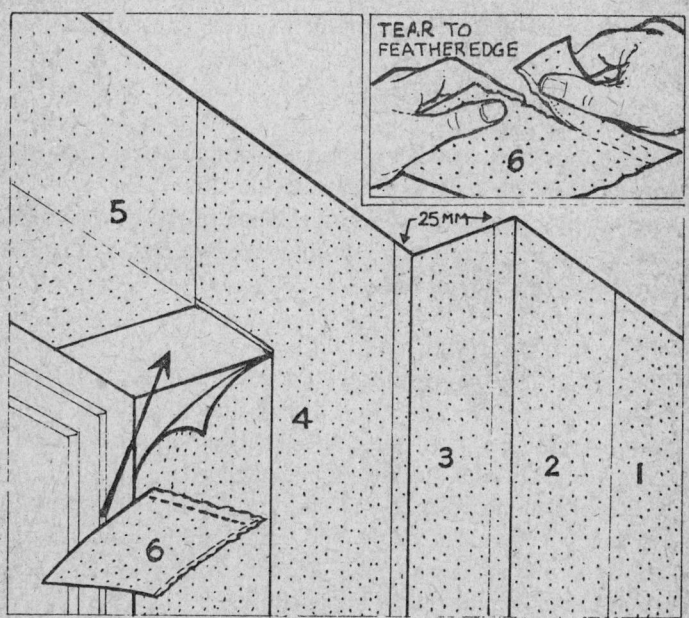

63. Order for papering into a reveal. Cut and feather in a piece in the corner where it will not be obvious.

When working inwards, hang the paper in the normal way, butt-join to the last section and cut at top and bottom so that the paper butts into the reveal. Leave a 6mm gap at the inside edge of the reveal and trim the paper round into this.

The next step is the same for both situations. Cut a further piece the length of the wall above the reveal plus the reveal, plus trimming allowance, matching for pattern. Align vertically and smooth round into the reveal.

Cut an oversize piece of paper to fill the gap left in the corner of the top reveal, again matching the pattern.

Trim to fit the reveal, but allow a 25mm edge overlap. Carefully tear a ragged, feathered edge on this overlap as this helps to camouflage the join when the paper is pasted into position.

Corners

Inner corners can be dealt with in one of two ways. One way is to offer up the length of paper to the corner and, with the back of the shears, crease-mark the line of the corner, then trim to this line. Paste and butt-joint the two pieces of paper together again.

Alternatively, measure the distance between the last full length and the corner. Add 25mm overlap, transfer this measurement to the width to be hung and cut off the excess. Hang with the 25mm overlap turned into the corner. Trim top and bottom, then butt-joint the two lengths together, again vertically with the pattern matched.

For projecting corners, measure the distance between the last full width and the angle, add 25mm, cut carefully along this line and hang, turning 25mm overlap around the corner. Butt-join the remaining portion.

Stair-well areas may present a problem, but tackle systematically, working from the main light source, or by

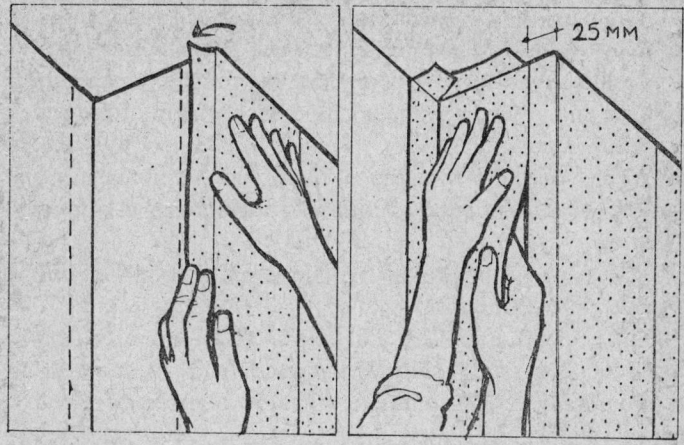

64. Projecting corners. Allow a 25mm turn on projections, for walls are often out of true, then trim to the vertical line.

65. Light switches, (Left). Cut a star segment, brush in and trim. First switch off power. (Right) Always brush out from the centre to the edges.

first hanging the longest length on the well wall where it adjoins the headwall, working outwards in both directions.

As a stair-well drop is heavy, use the concertina method of folding and get assistance to support the weight of the paper as you position it.

When you mark the vertical lines, allow a 25mm turn on to the headwall, plus overlaps for trimming at top and bottom.

Before papering around a light switch or power point, switch off at the mains.

Either loosen the fitting and trim behind it, or paper over it and cut back petal-shaped segments and trim carefully around the switch or point. Do the same for a ceiling rose.

Papering ceilings

You will need good access equipment when papering a ceiling, running the width of the room. Ideally, a trestle or two step ladders — bridged by a scaffold board. Position the access so that your head is about 250mm from the ceiling.

Hang the paper across the width of the room starting at the main window area and working back into the room. Chalk datum lines the width of the roll across the ceiling.

Cut out all the lengths required, allowing a 50mm overlap so that you can trim it into the wall angle. Paste as for wallpaper and concertina fold in 300mm loops. Use a spare roll of paper to support the length from underneath.

Start to apply the paper from one end, unfurl one fold at a time and smooth down each section as it is hung. Cut out round ceiling roses as for wall switches. Once all the area is papered trim off the excess at wall edges.

PLASTERWORK

Ceiling cracks
A cracked ceiling can be repaired by undercutting the cracks slightly and filling with cellulose filler, using a broad-bladed filling knife.

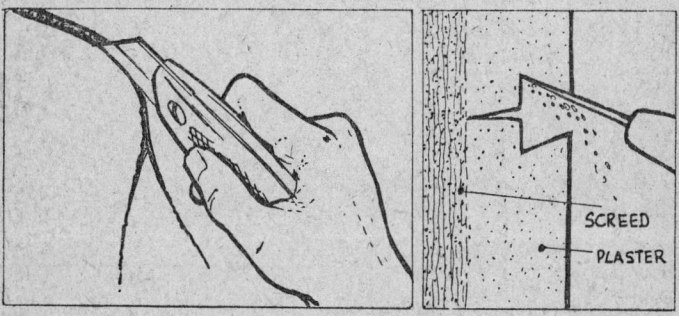

66. Cracks in plasterwork. When repairing a crack, undercut the hole before filling.

A firm but cracked ceiling can be disguised by lining with heavy-duty lining paper, then at right angles with woodchip or ingrain paper – see paperhanging. This can then be emulsion painted.

Modern ceilings consist of plasterboard with a plaster skin. In older houses, the ceiling may consist of lath and plaster. If the lath is not broken, a repair is usually possible.

Small holes

Patching plaster can be used to repair small holes. Larger holes can be filled with plaster-soaked paper, then finally filled with patching plaster, and rubbed down when dry.

Damage to plasterboard surfaces can be repaired by cutting back to sound plasterboard. Cover the hole with a piece of plastering scrim – which is made from jute.

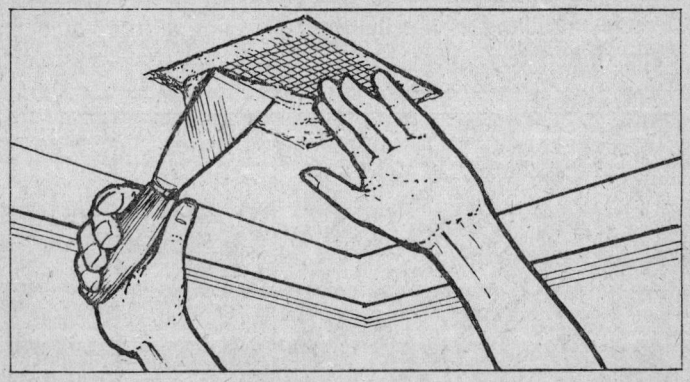

67. Small holes in plasterwork. Small holes in plasterboard can be covered with jute scrim and then with ceiling-board plaster finish.

Moisten the area with a damp brush and apply a thin plaster "slurry" around the edges with a filling knife. Press the scrim to this with the knife. Allow the plaster to "go off" slightly, then apply a thin skim coat over the scrim, feathered out on to the ceiling.

Allow to set partially, then flick water on to the area with a brush and smooth with even strokes of a steel finishing trowel, taking care to feather the edge. Glasspaper any slight irregularities, then paint.

Larger holes

Larger areas of ceiling damage may require repair with a section of ceilingboard. Cut out the damaged section back to a convenient joist, so that you can fix to half of each joist. At the ends you will have to nail in two cross-pieces or noggings for fixing.

Cut the new board with a 3mm all-round clearance and nail in, plaster (the darker) side downwards, with plaster-board nails at intervals of around 100mm.

Scrim the joints and replaster in the same way as for a small repair, then give two coats of emulsion paint. Emulsion allows the surface to "breathe" while the plaster is curing.

PLUMBING

Replumbing a home can be a daunting task – but if you carry out as much pre-preparation as possible, measuring cutting and fitting pipework before connecting to the supply and pre-plumbing the cold-water cistern and the hot-water cistern, you will minimise the time and dislocation involved in connecting up.

If you have to replumb the home fully, try to leave the kitchen tap and one toilet in service for as long as possible.

In older homes iron-barrel pipework and lead was widely used. In hard-water areas, the formation of lime scale can seriously restrict the bore of pipework. On hot-water services this can be dangerous. Old barrel pipe rusts and corrodes, and lead becomes brittle.

An old, rusting galvanised storage cistern is not worth patching up and may give trouble, culminating in a flood! An ancient hot-water tank will certainly be less efficient and much more costly to run than a modern hot-water cylinder.

Modern storage cisterns are made from glass fibre or from PVC. These are easily installed and will not deteriorate. Check, however, that your cold-storage and hot-water needs are adequate. As a rough guide, a three-bedroomed home needs a storage cistern of around 230 litres capacity. A larger home may need a capacity of 365 litres.

Copper and stainless steel are principally used in domestic plumbing. These tubes are easily cut with a small hacksaw. To cut pipe, first measure carefully, support the pipe firmly and cut with even strokes.

Square up the ends and slightly taper the outside with a flat file — this facilitates entry into a fitting. Use a round file to remove burrs from the mouth of the tube.

For the cold supply to kitchen and loft storage and its cold-feed outlet plastic plumbing can be used. It cannot, however, be used for hot-water services. Pipework is cut with a hacksaw and joined with solvent welding cement. There is the usual range of fittings, and you can also incorporate fittings such as stop cocks and gate valves. Because of the lower hydraulic drag of PVC, smaller pipe — 10mm instead of the usual 15mm copper pipe — can be used.

The most common fittings are the straight connector, the bend or elbow and the tee-piece. There is a variety of specialised fittings and variations on the main ones.

Stop cocks and gate valves can be connected into pipe runs on both metal and plastic plumbing.

Fittings are either compression-ended, where an "olive" or gland is compressed around the tube by the action of tightening the lock nut, or solder-joined. The latter is called a capillary joint and there are two types — a pre-soldered joint and the end-feed connector, to which you apply solder.

Insert the cut pipe filling into the mouth of the fitting, slide on the lock nut and the olive, and lightly smear non-toxic plumbing compound around the olive to consolidate the joint. Hand tighten, and then tighten a further half turn with a spanner. Avoid overtightening.

Clean the inside of the capillary fitting and the pipework with wire wool. Apply flux sparingly to the inside of the fitting and around the tube. There are some fluxes where tube cleaning is claimed to be less critical.

On a pre-soldered joint, push home the tube, then heat around the mouth of the fitting, using a butane blow torch, until a ring of solder appears evenly around the mouth of the tube. Lightly touch the joint with a piece of cored solder; this will consolidate the solder ring.

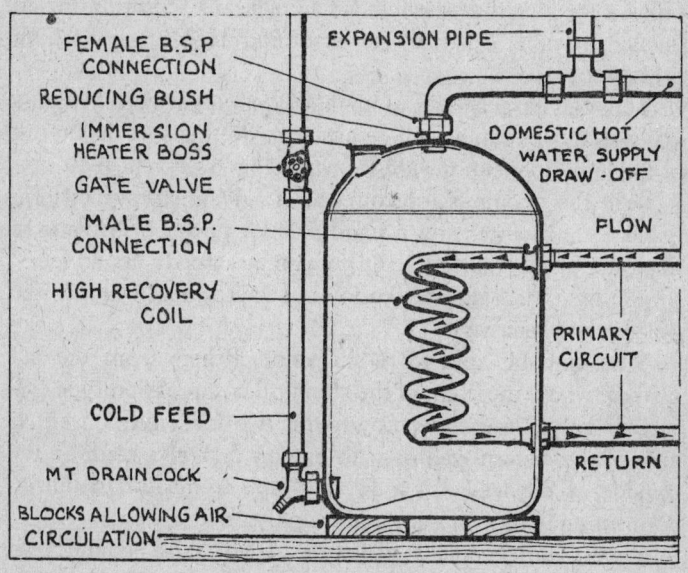

FEMALE B.S.P CONNECTION

REDUCING BUSH

IMMERSION HEATER BOSS

GATE VALVE

MALE B.S.P. CONNECTION

HIGH RECOVERY COIL

COLD FEED

MT DRAIN COCK

BLOCKS ALLOWING AIR CIRCULATION

EXPANSION PIPE

DOMESTIC HOT WATER SUPPLY DRAW - OFF

FLOW

PRIMARY CIRCUIT

RETURN

68. Layout of a typical hot-water cylinder.

Clean similarly for the end-feed fitting, connect, apply flux, then evenly heat the mouth of the fitting.

Apply solder to the mouth of the fitting until it will accept no more. Do not overheat when soldering or you may burn it and the joint will leak.

Where possible, avoid using fittings. These are expensive, and a possible source of turbulence.

You can save money by using a tool to bell the mouth of the fitting, clean this, and solder as for an end-feed fitting. While you may have to use elbow fittings in some circumstances, it is preferable to use a bending spring for small-bore pipework. You insert this into the tube, then bend the pipe over the knee.

Fix pipework with clips to the wall at intervals. Loose pipes can sometimes set up an unpleasant vibration called "water hammer" where the incoming mains are at high pressure.

You can largely preplumb a cold-storage cistern and a hot-water cylinder. It will be easier to do this sort of job out of the loft. Connections are shown in Fig. 68.

Drill the openings for connections in the storage cistern, using a tank cutter and a hand drill. A power drill tends to heat up plastic surfaces. Once you are ready to connect, drain down the old cistern, mop out the residual water in the bottom and remove it.

You may be able to re-use some fittings from the old cistern, where these are of the standard compression type.

Ball valves are either fitted with two lock nuts on either side of the cistern wall or with one on the valve stem on the outside of the wall. Fit a swivel "tap" connector to this to connect up with the rising-main supply.

Cistern outlets consist of flat or angled "tank" connectors, with a washer and a nut screwed to the inside wall. You may need one or two outlets — dependent on plumbing arrangements. A similar fitting is used for the overflow. The outlet should be placed well clear of wall surfaces.

Stand a PVC cistern on three 100mm × 50mm timbers, placed across the joists and a glass-fibre cistern on a continuous surface, such as 18mm blockboard. A lid keeps dust out.

Modern hot-water cylinders are usually made of copper, though some are made of glass-fibre. A standard cylinder is 915mm high × 450mm in circumference. It has a "dished" base to add strength. The top is "crowned" or domed to prevent airlocks.

There are three types — the direct, the indirect, and the self-priming cylinder. The direct cylinder is generally used with an immersion heater. The self-priming cylinder cannot be used for heating systems where the domestic hot water is pumped.

The indirect cylinder contains a heating coil, circulating heating hot water. This cannot mingle with the heated draw-off water. A direct cylinder can be converted into an indirect one by fitting a heating coil, resembling an immersion heater.

The self-priming cylinder separates the heating and draw-off waters by an air bubble. Pumping the water would disperse this.

Fittings to the hot-water cylinder are of the threaded variety, to which you fit bushes to connect the pipework. Wind PTFE sealing tape one and a half turns around the threads in an anti-clockwise direction. This provides a seal when the fitting is connected. Take care not to overtighten connections, for this can rupture the cylinder.

An expansion pipe must be taken up into the loft and curved above the cold storage cistern. Take this from the crown of the cylinder. Displace slightly from the outlet for the water will not then so readily expand. It is, however, seldom that hot water vents into the cistern. Stand the cylinder on two firm pieces of timber. This allows air to circulate beneath and prevents condensation from forming.

PLUMBING – FIRST AID

Bursts
Prevention is better than cure — make sure your loft or pipes are lagged so that the water in pipes cannot freeze, expand and cause bursts.

Bursts are more likely in older, leaded pipework. On modern copper tubing, the expanding ice will usually push a fitting apart, and this can usually be reconnected.

If you have a burst in lead pipework, it is well worth considering modernising by replacing with copper or stainless-steel tubing.

To repair a lead pipe it requires a skill called lead-burning. It really requires some practice to do successfully. For this you need a shave hook to clean up the metal, lamp black (applied to the joining pipe ends to limit the solder spread), blow torch, solder, plumber's metal, a wood cone or "dolly" to bell out the mouth of the pipe, a mole cloth, to wipe the joint, and tallow to lubricate it.

First, enlarge one end of the cut pipe, tapping and turning the cone or dolly in the pipe. Clean up the joining ends. You simply insert one end into the other, but if you have to bridge a burst by cutting out and inserting a piece of copper tubing, bell both ends.

Apply lamp black some 50mm back along the pipe. Flux, then tin the joining ends and connect. Heat and apply the plumber's metal, wiping to a neat feathered joint with the moleskin dipped in tallow.

If the burst is not too severe, you can probably tap the edges together and wipe the new joint over it.

Dripping taps

You should be able to shut off the incoming cold supply at the mains stop cock. There should also be gate valves to isolate various parts of the system. In some circumstances, you may have to tie up a ball valve, drain down a storage cistern and draw the crown of water off the hot-water cylinder.

The kitchen tap is the most likely to need attention, since it is the most used. To get at the inside of the tap, unscrew the head cover. This should be hand-tight, but if a wrench is

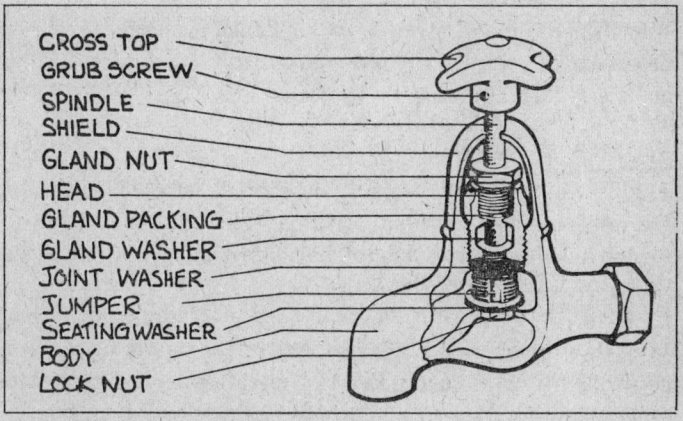

CROSS TOP
GRUB SCREW
SPINDLE
SHIELD
GLAND NUT
HEAD
GLAND PACKING
GLAND WASHER
JOINT WASHER
JUMPER
SEATING WASHER
BODY
LOCK NUT

69 Arrangement of a domestic tap.

needed, wrap a protective cloth round it. The headgear is beneath this. Loosen the hexagonal nut on the headgear to expose the washer on the valve seat.

On a low-pressure type – not usually the kitchen cold tap – it comes off with the spindle. The washer is secured to a brass "jumper" by a brass nut; remove the nut and fit the new washer. Check that it is suitable for either hot or cold water or both. You can use synthetic washers for either. Grease the threads when fitting the new washer to give ease of movement. Also grease the head-cover threads.

Where water bypasses the washer, the valve seat may need regrinding. However, you can fit a nylon washer and seating set over the existing valve seat to put this right.

Water trickling over the top of the tap heads suggests a leaking gland. Remove the tap handle, taking out the small locking grub screw. Unlock the gland screw and take out the old packing; replace this with cotton wool or string soaked in petroleum jelly.

Compress this into the stuffing box, but leave enough space for the gland screw to be tightened securely. Give one or two extra turns on the screw to consolidate against further leaks and reassemble.

Stop cock

This is your safety valve and you should test it occasionally. Do not leave it fully open, or it may bind and be difficult to turn in an emergency. Close by half a turn and grease the stem.

Cisterns

In both a flushing or a storage cistern, the supply of water is controlled by a float on an arm operating a shut-off valve. Once the water rises to a certain level, this closes the valve.

If the ball becomes damaged or water-logged it will not

rise and shut off the water, so the cistern will continuously overflow. A new valve is simply fitted by unscrewing the old and screwing on a new. An emergency repair can be effected by removing and draining the ball then replacing it inside a plastic bag.

A worn valve seating can be capped, as for a tap, with a nylon seating set. To replace a faulty inlet washer, pull out the split pin which holds the lever of the piston, which can then be removed. On some types, you may have to take out the cap at the end of the cylinder. Flush the valve seating clear of grit.

A faulty outlet washer means that you will have to tie up the ball arm, drain the cistern and bale out residual water. Undo the base nut on the flush pipe and the siphon, flush-lever linkage and the plunger disc can be removed. The washer can be simply changed by unscrewing a lock nut and the unit reassembled and replaced.

RAINWATER SYSTEMS

Rainwater systems, known collectively as rainwater goods, need regular inspection and prompt attention if any fault occurs.

Leaky guttering and down pipes can saturate the fabric of the home and penetrate inside. Blocked guttering can overflow and do much the same thing.

Scrape all débris from a blocked gutter, then flush clean with a hose. Lift out débris from the mouth of a down pipe, then flush thoroughly with the hose. You should fit a balloon to the opening, but chicken wire crumpled into a ball will do.

Broken or sagged gutter brackets need replacing or re-fixing. You may find the gutter seals have deteriorated.

Replace a damaged section of cast-iron guttering, if extensively rusted, with new. The seals usually consist of putty. Prise apart a leaking section, scrape out putty, rub down with a wire brush, treat for rust and reprime.

The putty should be fairly soft. Spread a layer, 6mm thick, evenly into the bottom, and press the sections firmly together, trim off excess with a piece of cloth.

Cut through rusted bracket bolts with a hacksaw, but treat first with a rust solvent to try to loosen them. Brackets may be screwed in or set in wooden plugs with "drive" nails.

When resetting displaced brackets, line these up with a cord line, fixed along the line of the brackets to ensure there are no dips. There should be a slight overall fall to the outlet.

Downpipes are often fixed by clips secured by "drive" nails. Lever the drive nails out with a case opener. You may have to dismantle the entire pipe section to remove these.

Loose joints between sections of a downpipe should be packed with non-hardening mastic. Push this into the joint with a putty knife and paint with a bitumen paint.

The other joint will be the shoe of the drainpipe (though the pipe may be jointed into drainage or a soakaway). This should be treated similarly.

A hole in cast-iron drainage can be repaired with glass fibre mat or a compound. Use these to manufacturer's instructions, cleaning the area and building up mat and resin in layers. Allow to dry, glasspaper smooth and repaint.

Try to avoid tackling these sort of jobs in wet weather — for obvious reasons!

Before repainting cast-iron guttering, clean with a wire brush to remove rust particles and treat with a rust inhibitor or paint with zinc-chromate primer.

The inside of the guttering can be painted with bitumen paint, once rust has been wire-brushed. Use a stiff brush to apply.

You can "marry" a cast-iron section of guttering to new plastic guttering — there are various makes of connector marketed.

You may find it best to use a portable access tower when repairing or replacing guttering.

If your guttering system needs replacement, it is easier to replace with lightweight PVC. This is relatively cheap, light, easy to handle and assemble, and does not deteriorate or need painting.

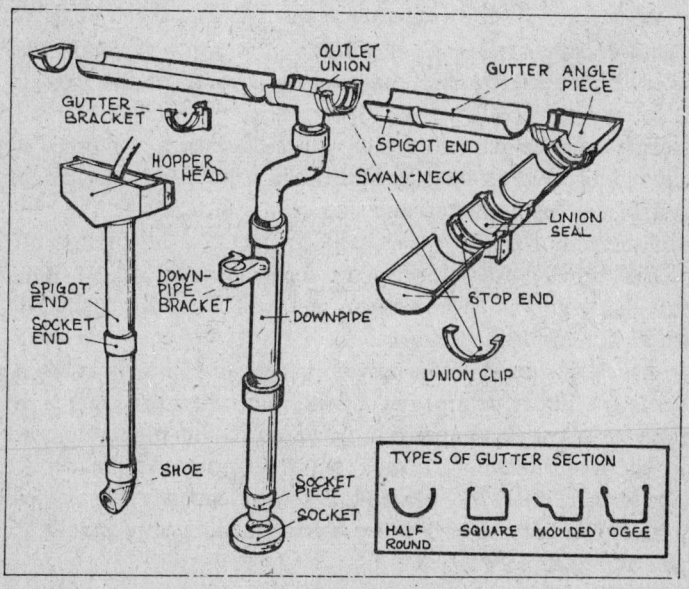

70. Rainwater system. The component parts of a rainwater system and types of guttering. You can also have square profile downpipes.

PVC guttering is generally made in grey, white or black in lengths of 4 metres and from 74mm to 150mm in diameter.

It is available in half round or square sections and has a better water-carrying capacity than cast iron.

Most types lap together with neoprene seals and clips to form a "dry joint". The most you may need to do is to replace a seal, if grit gets in and damages it.

Some types of guttering, but not downpipes, are joined using a cement-welding adhesive.

PVC guttering can be cut with a fine-toothed saw. Make cuts squarely so that sections seat squarely. Make sure your measurements are taken very carefully to avoid wasteful errors.

To check that you have all the parts you need and that everything goes together, make up the sections on the ground before fixing.

First, fix the gutter brackets. Place these so that there is a slight fall towards the downpipe. Fix a nylon string at one end of the fascia board and line up the brackets to this, so that there is no dip.

Fix brackets at three-metre intervals. Allow a 13mm expansion gap when joining up sections. There is usually an expansion mark to work to.

Brackets should not usually be more than 15mm away from a socket. Fix downpipes at a maximum of two metres. You need to allow for expansion upwards in the socket spigot.

Use a spirit level to ensure correct alignment and mark the uprights, in chalk, on the wall. Screw fix clips for downpipes with plugs, preferably between brick points. Screws should be sheradised or galvanised or plated.

The kit of parts which go to make up a guttering system is shown in Fig. 70. Angle sections are merely turned round to provide either an inside or an outside angle.

ROOFING

Slates and tiles
The condition of slates and tiles needs checking from time to time, for a leaking roof can cause a lot of damage. Whenever you tackle a roof repair, make sure that you use the correct access equipment, that it is sound and securely fixed, and that you use it correctly and safely. Avoid tackling roof jobs in icy, wet or windy weather.

You may be able to affect a temporary repair from inside the roof with heavy-duty polythene sheeting.

Slates
Slates can become worn and "layered" or damaged. You may be able to buy matching slates from a demolition site. If you take along a sample to a builder's merchants, you should be able to obtain what you need.

When buying second-hand slates, check carefully for hair-line cracks, flaking and powdering or layering – separation of the strata of the slate – and reject these.

Handle slates with care, for these are brittle. Never try to lift a pile of slates. Wear canvas gloves and carry under the arm.

Slates can be cut by marking with a trowel tip or a nail, then chopping along the line with the edge of the trowel. Cut halfway, then from the other end. Use a No. 8 masonry drill to make fixing holes for nailing; use an old slate as a template.

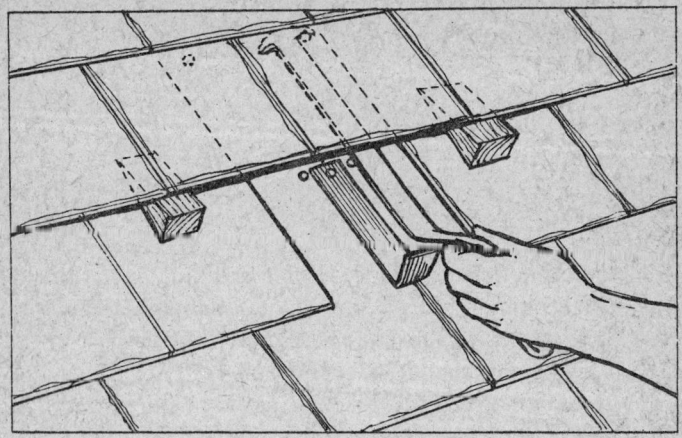

71. A ripper. This is used to pull out nails when removing slates or tiles.

To remove old slates, a tool called a ripper is required. This tool is best hired.

The head of the ripper is curved to hook round the nails holding the slates and rip them out. Use the ripper by sliding it beneath the slates above the one to be replaced.

Slates are staggered in adjacent rows so that any slate partially covers the two below it.

Fix slates with 25mm galvanised nails. A slater or tiler's hammer is a purpose-designed tool for the job.

To fix an individual slate, nail a clip of galvanised wire or copper strip through the lower slates, slide the replacement tile in, then bend up the end of the wire to support the inserted slate.

Tiles

Tiles are replaced in a similar manner to slates. Each course overlaps the course below. To remove a problem tile, you can

usually lift it with a trowel, push back slightly and then
withdraw it. Raise adjacent tiles slightly for this helps.

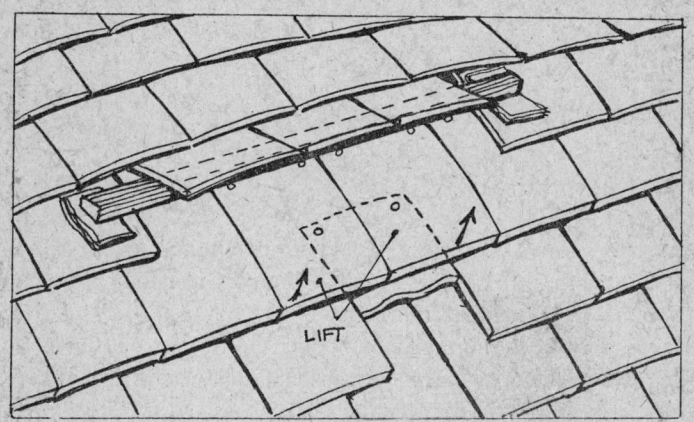

72. Removing a nailed tile. Wedge up those above for access.

If a tile is nailed, lift the two above it to expose the nails,
then pull these out.

Asbestos roofing

This is a brittle material, so never put your weight on it.
Asbestos cement consists of Portland cement and asbestos
fibre. Use chlorinated, rubber-based paint, but the surface
can be left unpainted.

Asbestos sheeting can be cut with a hard-point saw, but
always wear a face mask; *asbestos dust can be very harmful.*

Asbestos is easy to drill to take fixing bolts or drive
screws, but do not overtighten or you may crack the
material.

Acrylic and clear vinyl sheeting, like asbestos, is made in a
number of profiles and dimensions. It is easily cut with a

panel or tenon saw; support it firmly while cutting, so that it does not crack.

Clear plastic sheeting is similarly drilled for fixings.

SASH WINDOWS

Sash windows, correctly called double-hung sashes, work using cords, pulleys and weights. Usually, it is the sash cord which wears and needs renewal.

To replace a damaged or broken cord, you will have to remove both upper and lower sashes to get access to the cord or cords; there are two on each side.

First remove the fixing beads around the inside edge of the frame. Use a slim chisel to prise away a long bead in the centre, then smartly tap it back; the fixing pins will be proud of the bead and can then be removed easily.

Next, remove the parting bead between the sashes in a similar manner. Mark in pencil the position of the sash-cord ends on the front of the sash, with a corresponding mark on the frame.

Use pincers to remove the nails holding the sashcords. Hold the cords to stop the weights from falling behind the stile frame. Remove the inner sash and repeat the marking procedure on the other sash.

Unscrew or lever out the pocket covers. Remove the weights by pulling them through the pocket openings.

Buy pre-stressed wax cords for replacement.

In addition you need a length of string and a flat piece of lead, a weight called a "mouse". Roll this around the string to

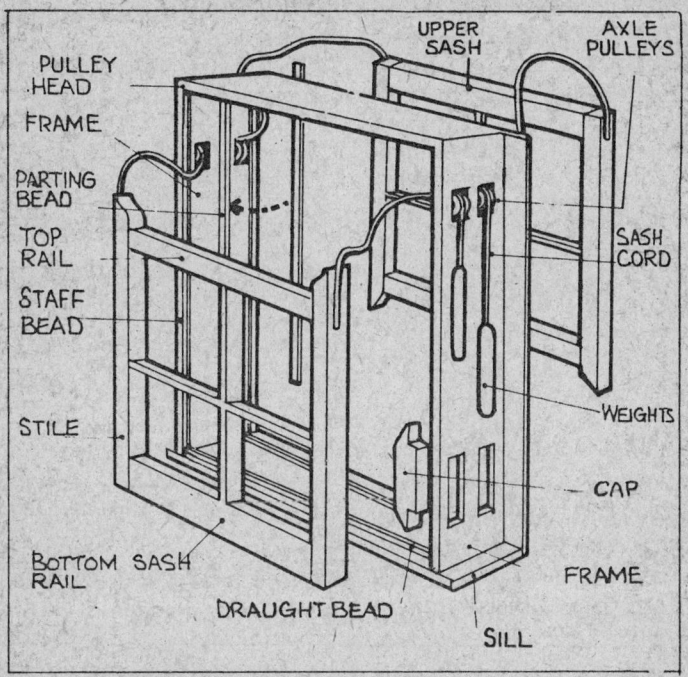

73. A double-hung sash window. General construction.

about the thickness of a cigarette but half the length, bending it slightly in the middle.

Feed the mouse over the groove of the outer pulley wheel until it falls behind the stile. Begin at the outer or upper sashcord.

Tie the new sashcord to the end of the string, pull this over the wheel and out through the pocket opening. The mouse can now be removed.

Next, tie the sashcords to the top of the weights, binding the loose cord end so that no knot or bulge can interfere with the opening of the window.

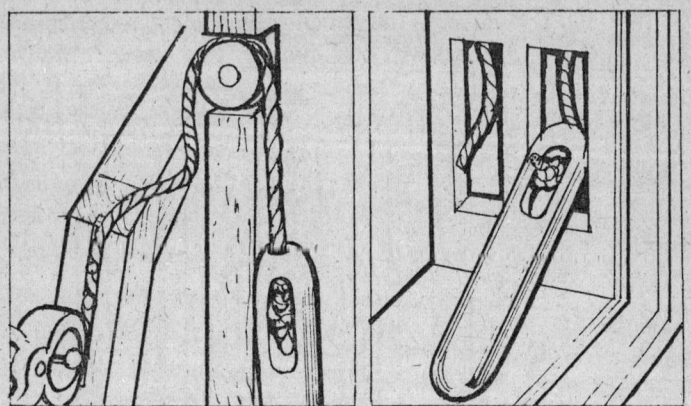

74. Replacing sash cords. Pull out the nails that fix the weight cords. Finally pull the weights out through the pocket pieces.

Bring the weights up some 50mm from the bottom and drive a nail half way through each cord into the pulley stile to hold them temporarily in place.

Cut each cord level with the pencil marks, and place the outer sash so that you can fit a cord into its groove.

75. Fixing the sash cord. Fix it with four or five "clout" nails.

Line the end up with the pencil mark on the edge of the sash and fix the cord with four or five "clout" nails, beginning at the pencil-marked point.

Once both cords are fastened, remove the temporary nails, and the stiles and sash can be lifted back in. Test by sliding the sash. Fit the weight in the inner or lower sash in a similar way, with the exception that the weights are pulled up almost to the pulleys.

SHOWERS

You can put a shower cubicle in a space of about only 760 sq. mm. Space on landings, deep cupboards, and recesses beneath stairs, in corners of bedrooms are among the points where you might feasibly fit a shower cubicle, subject, of course, to being able to provide the necessary services — hot and cold supply and drainage.

The most common possibility is to fit a shower or a shower attachment to the bath. The choice is between the shower mixer-tap, in place of existing bath hot-and-cold taps, and the fixed shower head, mounted above the bath.

With the shower mixer tap, you can choose between the shower and use of the taps, The arm can be fixed to choice in one or two positions to a pair of wall clips — either positioned for using the shower while sitting in the bath or at chest height. The flexible arm can also be hand-held. Some types fix to a clip over the taps, rather like a telephone on its cradle.

To stop water from splashing, a fixed screen, made from acrylic or similar material or a plastic curtain on rails needs to be fitted. You can buy proprietary units of both types which are simple to fit.

Shower cubicles come complete with all fittings. These just need connecting up.

The cold supply to a shower needs to be provided from the cold-storage cistern – and not from the mains. The hot water is usually supplied from a hot-water cistern. It is important that the pressures of these supplies should be as even as possible. The mains would provide far too high a pressure compared with storage hot water.

A shower used with a mixing set is best adjusted before getting into the bath. It is better, however, to use a thermo-static mixing valve. Though more expensive, these maintain the temperature settings regardless of any variations in pressure. This type of valve will usually enable variations in spray force to be made.

To work correctly, unless you incorporate an accelerator pump into the supply circuit, a minimum "head" or pressure of one metre is needed for a shower spray, usually a rose. A finer spray, which atomises the droplets even smaller than the rose, requires a head of 2.4 metres.

Increased head can sometimes be achieved by elevating the cold storage cistern in the loft. The "head" is the vertical distance between the outflow from the storage cistern to the shower outlet.

Plumb in the shower, using standard plumbing fittings. Usually, supply services can be run in 15mm copper tube. If there is a long pipework run involved or if there are a number of bends which reduce pressure, use 22mm pipework.

Try to ensure that the shower has "first pull" on the system. This means that it is the first connection on a circuit which may incorporate other taps and outlets. If possible, connect the shower up separately to the supply source.

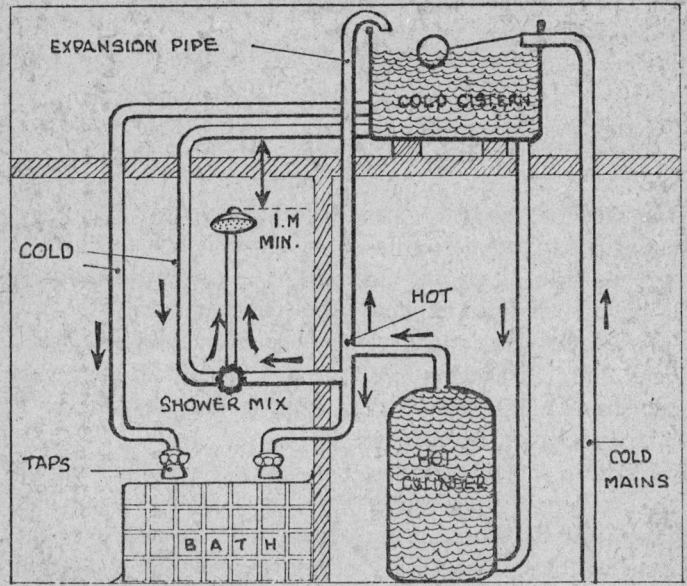

76. Showers. Diagrammatic layout of a shower, showing the minimum one-metre "head" or pressure of water needed for an effective spray.

The waste trap on a shower is similar to that on a bath and must have a minimum diameter of 38mm. A tubular trap is preferable to a bottle type as this is less prone to sedimentation and consequent blocking.

If you fit lighting in or near a shower, this must be of a fully enclosed, safety pattern and operated by a pull switch inside the room or switched from outside.

SILLS AND STEPS

Damaged sills and steps can let water penetrate indoors; a damaged step can also be dangerous, for it is easy to slip.

Repairs to either are carried out in a similar manner. Using a club hammer and a bolster, chip away the top 40mm. Make sure that the surface is clean and free from debris. Place timber shuttering firmly around to contain the repair mortar and to give a clean edge. Apply a dilute application of PVA liquid to the repair areas.

Mix one part of cement to four parts of soft sand and fill the opening. Use a wood float in a series of circular movements to distribute the repair concrete and level the surface. Make a slight forward slope to take water away, and slightly round the nose of the step or sill.

Allow the concrete to dry out for a couple of hours and polish smooth with a steel finishing trowel. Flick a little water on to the surface with a brush; this enables you to "plane" the trowel over the surface, without causing it to lift.

Small cracks can be repaired by slightly enlarging them, undercutting, bonding with PVA, then filling using a small pointed steel trowel.

STAIR REPAIRS

Creaky stairs can be irritating but this does not usually indicate any real hazard. It usually shows that a wedge under a tread has become loose. Wedges hold the treads and the risers (the uprights). Treatment with hammer and nails or screwdriver and glue will usually put this right.

A warped tread may cause creaking. Fix down firmly with countersunk screws.

Squeaking treads indicate side friction between the boards. Dust the joints with talcum powder or french chalk. Another possible cause may be loose glue blocks. These are triangular and usually glued and screwed in place. Tighten these up:

If a stair tread is cracked, reinforce this with a wood block or steel angle bracket if it is not possible to replace the tread.

Newel posts may work loose and you may have to take up a floorboard or two to rescrew the base. Posts are screwed to floor joists. If the joint between the post and the outer stair strings is loose, this also loosens all treads and risers. In this case, brace the post with wood blocks, glued and screwed into the inside corner.

TIMBER INFESTATION

Dry and wet rot and woodworm are the arch enemies of the timber structures in your home. Treatment must be prompt and the underlying causes eradicated.

Woodworm

Woodworm is a generic term for the larvae of several species of wood-boring beetles that can digest wood. These lay eggs on the surface of the wood, and the hatched grub bores into the timber, leaving no sign of entry, where it may stay for up to ten years.

When ready to pupate, the larva makes its way to just below the surface and the hatched beetle bores its way out leaving the tell-tale "frass' or dust and flight holes.

Structural timbers are best treated by one of the specialist woodworm-protection firms which give a 20-year guarantee.

Treatment for woodworm must be thorough, infected wood burnt and adjoining timbers treated.

A garden spray should be quite adequate to spray woodworm fluid or you can hire. Use a coarse spray with an extension line to reach awkward areas.

In a roof area spray joists, rafters, and purlins. Saturate the timbers. The amount of fluid depends on the size of your roof and the dryness of the timber.

Clean all timber before treating it. Cover the cistern and either cover or remove roof-insulation materials, such as lagging. Also cover any electrical cables. Wear old clothes, gloves and, for safety, goggles and a light fume mask. Do not use a naked light while spraying.

When treating floorboards take up and burn infected timber. Lift every fourth board, so you can treat the under sides of the boards and the joists.

Floors can take up to six months to dry out so use a temporary floorcovering or lay a sheet of polythene over the boards.

If fluid stains plaster, apply an aluminium primer before redecorating.

Dry rot

Dry rot, living fungi, which feed on the wood and turn it to a weak, dry, "friable" shell, thrive in damp and poorly ventilated conditions.

Your attack must be on both cause of the damp such as lack of air circulation, and the areas of decayed timber. Dry rot causes the surface of the timber to bulge.

One of the most vulnerable areas is under the floorboards. Check regularly for decay and if you find signs of attack make a systematic search of the area.

Work outwards to a radius of about a metre from the point of attack until you are clear of further decay.

Remove all the rotted timber at least a metre beyond it and burn it. Where structural damage is involved you may need to get specialist help.

Treat replacement timber with a wood preservative. Pay particular attention to joist ends and paint with bituminous paint, and, at the same time, spray round adjoining timbers up to 1.50m away from the cut-out sections.

Fungi can also attack plaster and brickwork. Remove the plaster and treat the walls with a fungicidal solution. Drill spaced staggered holes in the surface to allow dry-rot fluid to saturate the area.

Then working down the wall, apply a fungicidal solution to saturate the brickwork. Where the fungi have penetrated the wall treat both sides.

Allow to dry out before re-rendering. A 6mm coat of zinc-oxychloride plaster can be applied between the render and finish coats if you replaster.

Wet rot

This is also caused by a fungal growth but requires moister conditions to survive. It will attack plaster and wood. Test timbers by pushing a knife into the surface. Cut out and burn the affected wood and replace with timber treated with two coats of dry-rot fluid.

Also treat surrounding timbers, plaster and brickwork. Wet rot is easier to cure than dry rot for once the source of damp is removed the rot stops.

TOOLS

Always buy the best tools you can afford; a few good, versatile tools are better than a greater number of inferior ones. The latter will give poorer results, and may break or wear out quickly.

Good tools are expensive, but you can spread the financial load by budget-plan buying. Buy one or more new tools each week or month. Your tools will quickly grow into a comprehensive kit.

Keep tools in storage boxes, protect them and ensure that they are always readily to hand. Use tools only for their intended purposes. Keep cutting edges sharp and protect all tools from the effects of damp.

Saws
The panel saw is intended for finished work but can be used for ripping, cutting down the grain or cross-cutting across the grain. A good average saw is one about 550mm long with 10 points (teeth) to each 25mm of length.

A handyman's knife can accept a wide variety of blades, from keyhole type to laminate cutter.

Saws with Teflon-coated blades, cut best through resinous or damp timber. The tenon or back saw is needed for finer work. This has a stiffened backing to ensure a straight cut. A 250mm 14-point saw is a good choice.

Vices
To hold materials firmly when cutting, the vice is the basic holding tool. A portable vice is a useful item, for it can be clamped on to a range of firm surfaces. Clamps can also be used to hold things together.

Drills
A hand drill plus a variety of wood and masonry twist bits covers most drilling needs. For making larger holes use a hand or bit brace. This is used with centre bits and augurs. The brace can be used in countersinking.

A power drill capable of drilling at slow speeds in masonry and hard surfaces is a good alternative (see also power tools). Twist bits used in power tools differ from those used in hand drills.

Planes
A medium smoothing plane about 250mm long takes care of planing timber on the bench to easing doors and windows.

Planer-files and rasps are of various types, from block to hand plane.

Measuring and marking
A marking gauge is used for marking or scribing a line parallel with the edge of a board before cutting or chiselling. The mortice gauge is used for marking out woodworking joints. A metal rule, about 600mm long, also provides a useful straight edge. A retractable steel rule is used for measurements of greater length.

A try-square is required to mark out accurate right angles.

The combination try-square enables you to mark accurate 45° angles as well as right angles. Use a marking knife to mark out, for a pencil is not precise enough.

Hammers
Hammers include pin, tack and claw hammers. The 450-gram weight claw hammer is the best general-purpose choice. You can use the claw to withdraw nails or prise up floorboards.

Screwdrivers
There are two basic types of screw head, the conventional slotted type and the star-headed type which has a series of radial slots in the head, called Pozidriv. The advantage is that the Pozidriv screwdriver is less likely to slip and damage the surface of the material.

Chisels
The two main types are the firmer chisel, for all types of work, and the bevel-edged chisel, a lighter type, for finer work. A set of three bevel-edged chisels, such as a 6mm, 12mm and 25mm, will cover most needs.

Spirit level
This is to check horizontal and vertical levels. A level about 1 metre long is best.

Work aids
A bench hook, which is easy to make, is used to hold timber firmly when cutting with a tenon saw. This consists of a baseboard and two battens at each end at top and bottom. Battens are slightly shorter than the base width, so that you do not cut through them. The board is reversible.

Tool care

Keep chisels and plane irons sharp. Badly worn cutting edges may need regrinding on a carborundum wheel to restore the edge. Remove pitted surfaces before sharpening on a fine stone, then honing.

Inspect tools regularly for sharpness and damage to cutting edges, for you may otherwise cause damage to the work you are doing.

Painting

You will need a good set of real-bristle paint brushes in a range of sizes. Paint rollers and paint pads complement or provide an alternative. Also needed are various grades of glasspaper and wet-and-dry production paper, plus a sanding block, a butane gas torch and stripping knives. Always clean brushes carefully and store in a dry place after use.

Plumbing

A standard and a junior hacksaw. Use high-speed steel blades when cutting. A flat file and a round file are required for removing burrs from ends of cut pipework. Two good adjustable spanners, bending springs and a pipe cutter (the latter an optional extra).

Glazing

A putty knife and a wheel glass cutter.

Electrics

A pair of cutters, round-nosed pliers, an insulated screwdriver and, optionally, a neon-tester. The latter glows when inserted into the live side of a socket. Also, hang a card of fuse wire beside the consumer unit.

Power tools

The electric drill is the basic power tool. This can accept a variety of attachments to make it more versatile.

Attachments can convert a drill into, among other things, a power saw, a jig-saw or an orbital sander and power a bench lathe. It is preferable to buy integral tools which are purpose-designed.

Buy the best drill you can afford. Do not use a fixed-speed power drill for cutting holes in concrete. Use one with a slow-speed facility or, best of all, a hammer-drill.

Power planes are now also made for the domestic market.

WALLCOVERINGS

Decorative wallcoverings, from paper to felt, hessian and cork are able to provide an interesting range of surface finishes.

The most popular wallcovering is the standard flat-printed paper, produced in a wide range of colourways and designs.

Vinyl-coated paper has a thin PVC coating which makes it tough, hard-wearing and easy to clean. It is made in a wide choice of colours and designs, and you can get high sheen, matt or even metallic finishes. This is excellent in hallways, kitchens and bathrooms but where there may be condensation it must be hung with a fungicidal paste. Some vinyl papers are pre-pasted.

Washable papers, which have a thin resin coating, and with gloss or matt surfaces, are among the best for kitchens and bathrooms, or where you want a spongeable surface. When hanging in areas of high condensation use a fungicidal paste. In other areas, use a proprietary cold-water paste, starch-and-flour glue or tub glue.

Ingrain or woodchip papers have a textured effect and are excellent on sound, but blemished surfaces. The texturing looks attractive and the surface can be painted to choice. Use a fungicidal paste if you intend to paint the paper. These papers can also be bought pre-finished.

Embossed papers will give a raised textured finish. Line the walls horizontally and use a thick paste to apply. Avoid flattening the embossed surface when brushing out.

Flock papers are heavy and have a velvet-like pile finish. Some have a vinyl finish. Take care when smoothing down not to damage the surface. Use a roller covered with a soft material such as baize or chamois leather.

Hessian

Hessian wallcovering, backed or unbacked, is made from jute. When hanging unbacked hessian, line the walls horizontally with matching lining paper, then if the joints do spread slightly they will not be so noticeable. Unbacked hessian is more difficult to hang; use a heavy-duty paste to hang and a felt roller on the seams.

Linen, backed or unbacked, is an attractive textured material. Hang backed linen in the same way as ordinary wallpaper, and unbacked linen on to a pre-pasted wall.

Cork paper, consisting of thin sheets of cork or cork shavings bonded on to a paper backing, offers another choice of textured surface. Hang with a PVA adhesive.

ZINC

This is used for flashings or soakers but is not among the most durable of materials; it will wear out in time. An effective repair can be made by applying a proprietary mastic-backed aluminium strip. These have either a bright-aluminium or a leaded finish.

INDEX